DIALOGUES

— with a —

MODERN MYSTIC

DIALOGUES

— with a —

MODERN MYSTIC

ANDREW HARVEY

— and —

MARK MATOUSEK

The Theosophical Publishing House
P.O. Box 270
Wheaton, IL 60189-0270

A publication of the Theosophical Publishing House,
a department of the Theosophical Society in America.

*This publication made possible with
the assistance of the Kern Foundation*

Library of Congress Cataloging-in-Publication Data

Harvey, Andrew, 1952-
    Dialogues with a modern mystic / by Andrew Harvey and Mark Matousek
       p.   cm.
    ISBN 0-8356-0704-6 : $12.00
    1. Spiritual life,   2. Harvey, Andrew, 1952—Interviews,
  3. Mysticism.   I. Matousek, Mark.   II. Title.
BL624.H344   1994
291.4'22—dc20   94-12333
                                                          CIP

Book Design by Beth Hansen

9 8 7 6 5 4 3 2 1 * 94 95 96 97 98 99

This edition is printed on acid-free paper that meets the
American National Standards Institute Z39.48 Standard

Printed in the United States of America by Versa Press

To the Mother

ACKNOWLEDGMENTS

ANDREW HARVEY WOULD LIKE TO THANK HENRY AND LEILA LUCE FOR *their wonderful hospitality and generosity which made this book possible.*

MARK MATOUSEK THANKS STEPHEN BODIAN, RAY GRASSE, HOWARD Morhaim, Brenda Rosen, Deborah Treisman and John White *for editorial help; Eve Ensler, Barbara Graham, Robert Levithan, Christie Cox, James Thornton, James Lecosne and Amy Hertz for moral support; Louis Morhaim for staying; and most of all, the memory of Carole Snyder, who watched this grow while she disappeared.*

The most beautiful and profound emotion we can experience is the sensation of the mystical. It is the sower of all true science. He to whom this emotion is a stranger, who can no longer wonder and stand rapt in awe, is as good as dead.

—Albert Einstein

The 21st century will have to be mystical or not at all.

—Andre Malraux

Vuelvete, paloma,
que el ciervo vulnerado
por el otero asoma,
al aire de tu vuelo, y fresco toma.

(My dove, turn back,
for now the wounded stag
is climbing up the slope,
freshened by the breeze of your flight.)

—St. John of the Cross

CONTENTS

PREFACE

LATE ONE AFTERNOON IN AUGUST, 1991, ANDREW HARVEY AND I WERE invited to hear a talk at the New Camaldoli monastery in Big Sur, California. The speaker was Father Bede Griffiths, the late Benedictine monk and author who devoted his life to the founding of a Christian-Hindu ashram in south India and to the rapprochement of the world's mystic traditions. Knowing Bede only from his writings, I was shocked upon entering the small chapel by his otherworldly beauty, gaunt as an El Greco saint, snowy-haired in a saffron robe. In flawless Oxbridge tones, he proceeded to speak for an hour on a topic that didn't interest me—contemplation in daily life, or something equally as dull—then turned, unexpectedly, to a personal experience that recently shattered his own spiritual understanding.

Seated outside his ashram hut one morning before dawn, Bede told us, he was suddenly knocked to the ground by an invisible force during meditation. Frightened, he managed to crawl to his bed, where he remained for a week in a semi-conscious state, attended by doctors unable to diagnose his condition. After ten days, the doctors were beginning to give up hope. Last rites were administered. Then one afternoon when Bede lay there dying, a voice came to him, whispering the following words, "Remember the Mother." He recovered shortly afterward.

Andrew and I were stunned. Here was one of the great mystic pioneers of our time, a devout Christian who had spent the past fifty years working for spiritual reform, admitting a major oversight in his faith. It is the Mother, Bede went on to say, who is the source of creation and whose force is now being loosed upon the world. It is the Mother whose grace is so sorely needed by the Church, to help it enfold a suffering world, to quiet its fundamentalism, dissolve its bureaucracies and heal this ailing planet.

When Bede's talk was finished, Andrew and I sat on a cliff overlooking the Pacific. The sun had almost set behind a bank of golden clouds; we, saying nothing, watched the light play on the dark water. All this is the Mother, I thought, thinking about what the monk had said, sinking into an open-eyed trance. I saw myself floating in her glass belly, gazing out onto a magical world of fantastic color and leaf sounds, being given an experience of what a moment in her might be, the rapture of it. The eucalyptus, the boulders jutting out of the black water, the gulls and pelicans and seals squalling in the increasing dark: all of these things revealed themselves to me in that moment as her. This experience was not imaginary or symbolic, but a tangible presence, a suffusion. I was breathing her, being carried within her breath. The world seemed to expand and contract with my own lungs, or to dissolve; I couldn't tell. When Andrew left, I stayed there for a long time, staring out into this heaven.

"What do I need to know?" a voice inside me finally asked.

"Only love," she answered.

This book is about that love and the revolution of the Mother taking place in our time. It argues for the return of the Divine Feminine to the forefront of worldwide spirituality and for the sublime potential of enlightenment as the cornerstone of human life, to heal our patriarchal sickness and inspire—at this crucial moment—a total change of heart.

This transition must begin with the understanding that every human being is a mystic in his or her own right. Tragically, ours is the first "great" civilization to deprive its people of this truth; the first, despite its pop and fundamentalist religiosity, not to offer as the highest station of human life the states of unity, wisdom, compassion and grace which come through transcendental experience. As these dialogues will demonstrate, the effect of this denial on every aspect of our global crisis has been devastating and complex.

Andrew Harvey is one of the foremost spokespersons for this mystic renaissance and for the return of the sacred feminine to Western culture. Himself a mystic, the Anglo-Indian poet and scholar is unique among contemporary writers on spirituality, speaking, as he does, not from some academic distance, or even from the cautious position of a conscientious practitioner, but with the full splendor of the mystic heart on fire for the Beloved. In his extraordinary lectures and written works—particularly the "re-creations" of quatrains by the Sufi master Jalalludin Rumi and the confessions of his mystic initiation by Mother Meera in *Hidden Journey*—Andrew has helped to infuse into our contemporary mystic literature the passionate abandon of illumined, personal testimony.

This has happened less by choice than as an inevitable outpouring of the author's extreme, and particular biography. Born in 1953, Andrew was raised in Delhi during the twilight of the Raj. He spent his childhood in a household which, though Christian, was actually a crossroads of many faiths, filled with Moslem and Hindus, holy men and women saints who laid foundations of wonder and sacredness in the child's imagination. At the age of nine, this connection was broken when Andrew was sent to school in England, an experience he likens to being "closed up in a refrigerator." While this exile traumatized the strange and brilliant boy, it also served a deeper purpose, opening the wound of separation—from Mother India, from sacred culture—that would propel him later into a spiritual homecoming.

He excelled, nevertheless. At Oxford, Andrew won the highest honor in
the English meritocracy as the youngest Fellow of All Souls College at
the age of twenty-one. As an historian, poet and Shakespearean scholar,
he became famous for his renegade brilliance and mad-bad poet
eccentricities, as well as for his intimacy with literary *eminences gris* such
as Isaiah Berlin, Iris Murdoch and W.H. Auden. Unfortunately, the cost of
this excellence was dangerously high. At twenty-five, suicidally disillu-
sioned by bloodless, godless, English life, desperate to escape this
"concentration camp of reason," Andrew returned to India. There, on
Christmas Day, 1978, he met Mother Meera in the seaside town of
Pondicherry and began the long and difficult process of initiation that he
recorded, thirteen years later, in *Hidden Journey*.

Following the book's publication, I interviewed Andrew in New York
about the exact nature of his mystic experiences. We'd met five years
earlier when I was a fast-track magazine editor in New York City (a
meeting which changed my life and led me first to Germany—where my
lifelong skepticism was severely altered by meeting Mother Meera—then
on a journey with Andrew to the Himalayas and south India). The tran-
script of this first conversation was published in several magazines and
prompted a large and enthusiastic response from readers who seemed
to warm to the balance of our contrary voices—poet and journalist,
visionary and skeptic, balloon and string. It was this enthusiastic
response that inspired us to expand our conversation to book length.

The dialogues themselves took place over the course of two, fourteen-
day marathons in California and Germany. They are modeled after the
Sufi tradition known as *sohbet*, literally the spiritual talk of friends. This
style of informal investigation between brothers and sisters on the path
is, we believe, central to the way of the Mother, free of dogma, authority, hierarchy or conclusion. Taking this ideal to heart, we followed our
topics as they presented themselves and were often surprised by the
intensity of the atmosphere created between us. More than once, we

shared identical visions. On several occasions, we noticed, at the same moment, a strange, milky "light" appearing in the room. With comic regularity, we were led "accidentally" to a quotation—from Rumi, Nisargadatta, the *Flower Ornament Sutra* or St. John of the Cross—that precisely illustrated a point we were discussing. Throughout our time together, Andrew and I were reminded of Christ's assertion that when two or more are gathered in God's name, miracles begin to happen. Strange as this may sound to Western ears, it was absolutely clear from the beginning of these dialogues that the process taking place between us was guided by the Mother herself, whose force—like a wind on water—carried us forward to our destination.

For the sake of clarity, we have ordered this free-flowing movement into a four-part composition, corresponding to the following four questions: Where is the human race today? Where are we going? How will we get there? What will we find? Thus, our talks progress from a necessarily harsh analysis of the "concentration camp of reason," to a description of the Mother's way (and the future evolution of humankind envisioned by Sri Aurobindo), to a discussion of the ways and means of spiritual life and, finally, to a brief description of the mystic tenets of darkness, silence and nonduality.

As the Dalai Lama and many other contemporary spiritual leaders have emphasized, ours is not an era when seekers after God can afford to withdraw from the world. As darkness and danger increase around us, enlightenment becomes less and less a private affair. We are being called upon today to act as enlightened revolutionaries, bodhisattvas of compassionate action to preserve the creation and to help usher in the next millennium. It is with this urgent hope for transformation and as a manifesto of radical confidence that we offer these dialogues to the reader.

Mark Matousek
New York City
January, 1994

INTRODUCTION

God does not proclaim Himself. He is everybody's secret.

—Katha Upanishad

This is our destiny, to be one with God in a unity which transcends all distinctions, and yet in which each individual being is found in his or her integral wholeness.

—Bede Griffiths

All mystics come from the same country and speak the same language.

—St. Martin of Tours

It's not the earthquake that controls the advent of a different life but storms of generosity and visions of incandescent souls.

—Pasternak

MM: *What is your definition of a mystic?*

AH: A mystic is someone who has direct cognition of God beyond thought or image. A mystic is one whose eyes have been opened through purification, discipline and grace to the living mystery and lives consciously in the divine presence. As the great Sufi mystic Ibn 'Arabi wrote, "He who knows himself does not see other than God, and he who does not know himself has not seen God." All cultures at all times have had their mystics who have

known the supreme secret that God is in us and we are in God
as a part of God, and who have owed their spiritual health to the
reality of wisdom and love which the mystic directly awakens.

MM: *Why then is mysticism viewed so skeptically by our culture?*

AH: Because our culture glorifies reason and science, both man-
made and limited forms of knowing, and because there are two
fundamental and dangerous misconceptions about the mystic.
The first is that mysticism in some way denies the world. This is
untrue. The mystic sees the world for what it is—the theater of
divine grace—and sees it with gratitude and rapture.

The second misconception is that mystics are weak, passive,
abstracted and impotent. The opposite is the case. Many of the
most heroic and active figures in history, from the Buddha to
Lao Tzu, from Christ to Gandhi, from Dante to Einstein, have
been mystics whose creativity, stamina and altruistic action
have been fuelled by divine knowledge and energy.

MM: *All of which are painfully needed in this dangerous time.*

AH: This is, in fact, the darkest time in human history. At all dark
times, it has been the mystics who have carried forward the
sacred knowledge so that the human race would not forget its
inner divinity. When the great Buddhist monasteries in India
were destroyed in the eleventh and twelfth centuries, certain
monks endured intolerable hardship to see that their wisdom
did not perish. In the fourteenth century when the Mongols were
destroying the Islamic world, Rumi summed up in his life six
hundred years of Sufi inquiry. At a degraded moment of the
Roman Empire, Christ was born with the message of love that
was an attempt to transform history. As the night of materialism

settled on the West from the seventeenth century onwards, certain hidden alchemists and visionaries, artists such as Blake, Novalis and Whitman, struggled to keep alive a sacred vision of humanity. In the decadence of Hinduism in the late nineteenth century, saints like Ramakrishna and Aurobindo arose to give to India and the world incandescent examples of the genius of the Hindu soul. Today, great figures such as the Dalai Lama, Mother Teresa, Thich Nhat Hanh and the late Bede Griffiths—as well as many uncelebrated mystics of all kinds and creeds living so-called ordinary lives all over the world—are in their different ways witnessing the mystic truth that must not be allowed to die.

This truth of our divine identity is not a luxury for a few adepts but is *essential* now for the survival of the human race. At a time when all other visions have failed us, the mystical vision offers hope for a great transformation that is the destiny of the human race if we now have the courage to reach for it.

Part One

1

THE CONCENTRATION CAMP
OF REASON

MM: *You've begun by calling this the darkest age in human history. To some, this may seem an exaggeration.*

AH: Our unwillingness to face the extremity of the situation is part of the problem. We are certainly at the end of a civilization, a whole cycle of history, and, possibly, at the end of the world. The facts of our global crisis—a crisis that is at once political and economic, psychological and environmental—show us clearly that the human race has no hope of survival unless it chooses to undergo a total change of heart, a massive, quite unprecedented spiritual transformation. Only the leap into a new consciousness can engender the vision, moral passion, joy and energy necessary to effect change on the scale and with the self-sacrifice necessary to save the planet in the time we have. The message we are being sent by history can be summed up in four words: transform or die out. Many experts agree that we have, at the most, fifteen or twenty years left before extreme crisis becomes unalterable catastrophe. Teilhard de Chardin wrote, "Humanity is being taken to the point where it will have to choose between suicide or adoration." I have no doubt that we are at that point now. Human survival depends on whether we are brave enough to face the full desolation of what we have done to our psyches and the planet, and wise and humble enough to turn to the Divine inside and outside us to learn what we will need to go forward.

The last time I saw the great Catholic mystic and visionary Bede Griffiths, just before he died, he blessed me and said, "The hour of God and mankind's greatest ordeal is now here." "Can we get through?" I asked him. "The mercy and the help of God is always stretched out to us, always," he said, "even now at this late hour. But we must be humble enough to ask for them. Everything depends on whether we can abandon our pride before it is too late."

MM: *I don't disagree with a word of what you're saying. But isn't it also true that apocalyptic scenarios have always been around?*

AH: This is not an apocalyptic scenario, not a "scenario" at all, in fact. It is where we are; it is what is happening; it is terrifying, and anyone not in a trance of denial knows it. No amount of wishful thinking and sophisticated drawing of pseudo-historical parallels can make this agony go away.

It is hard enough for a human being to face the fact of his or her own mortality. What we have to face now is not merely our own death, but the possible death of everything and everyone we love, the holocaust of nature herself, the mother we have ignored and betrayed for so long. If we do not face our present danger in all its horror without consolation or illusion, we will never find in ourselves the passion and courage necessary to change. Catastrophe can become grace, and disaster possibility, only if we use their own energy against them by accepting what they have to teach us and acting with complete sincerity to transform ourselves.

Last year, I was in Bodh Gaya, meditating near the place of the Buddha's enlightenment. These words of the Fire Sermon came to me: "Monks, all is burning…The eye is burning, visible forms are burning…Burning with what? Burning with the fire of lust, burning with the fire of hatred, burning with the fire of delusion." As I heard these words inwardly, I saw in my mind's eye a forest in the Amazon erupt in flames; the vast flame-burst of Hiroshima; the blaze of a gas oven in a concentration camp; gutted and burning huts in Somalia, Angola, Cambodia; the charred and smoking hills around Sarajevo. And I saw and understood with an intensity and grief I had never before been strong enough to bear the full horror of what this century has accomplished.

MM: *Your spiritual training did nothing to mitigate this pain?*

AH: On the contrary, awakening brings with it a heightened sensitivity to pain. No true mystic is sentimental. I know very well the evil in myself, so I know that the inner world of humankind's psyche has always been on fire with lust, delusion and hatred. These fierce powers have created terror and destruction throughout recorded history, with only a very few periods of relative calm. What makes our contemporary situation so particularly menacing is that these powers in us now have at their disposal a range of lethal technologies that can do anything. Now, the external world is burning to death in the fires of our inner madness.

MM: *In other words, evil is not increasing, only its tools.*

AH: This century has seen a quantum leap in the powers that our evil has at its command. A medieval Mongol or ancient Roman on a horse could, on a good day, kill fifty women and children and burn down a village or two. A ruthless modern dictator—with which the modern world is swarming—can wipe out a country before breakfast. Greedy and amoral people have always done harm, but now, with the power of the media being as universal as it is, a handful of unscrupulous and cynical moguls can trivialize and deaden the minds of billions and darken the course of a whole civilization. The massacres of the past, though filled with every form of cruelty (read Herodotus or Tacitus), did not menace all existence down to the last dolphin and mouse and fern.

MM: *This destruction extends beyond the physical world into our hearts, minds and souls.*

AH: Yes. There has always been in the human psyche a tendency to rage against wisdom and its demands, but this tendency has escalated through technology and mind control to what can only be called a genocide of wisdom. The Chinese have decimated Tibet, the home of what may be the supreme wisdom culture humankind has seen. Industrial "progress" has fundamentally threatened indigenous people all over the world—from the Hopis to the Yamomamis to the Inuits, from the Kogis to the Todas to the Australian Aborigines—who have preserved against insuperable odds and over stretches of time the sacred ancestral knowledge of our species. We have silenced many of the gentle, patient voices that could have warned or guided us at the very moment when we need their inspiration most.

MM: *What's more, we conspire subtly with this genocide through fatalism in the face of so much bad news.*

AH: A friend of mine was one of the survivors in a plane crash. He described the last few minutes before the plane hit the moun-

tain. During the first five minutes, as people realized the end
was coming, they screamed, sobbed and prayed out loud. In the
next two minutes, this subsided and finally, at the end, people
just sat there numb, frozen to their seats. I often think that many
people feel themselves to be in those last few minutes, too
stunned even to cry out. So much in our official culture con-
spires with this passivity; its relentless trivialization of serious
issues, its passion for distraction, its fanatical, irrational belief
in reason and the power of science to explain away *everything*,
prevent us from facing where we are and what we do. The
liberals announce calmly the death of Satan at the very moment
when the Satan in us is having an orgy of universal destruction.
The ozone layer is gaping over Alaska and South America and
Australia, while the papers are full of photographs of Madonna's
latest bullet bra. Thousands of irrecoverable and sacred species
of animals, plants and insects vanish each month, and all the
media has been excited by this week is whether Hillary Clinton
has insulted the dignity of peas. A billion or more people live on
less than a dollar a day in conditions of desperate misery, while
Hollywood goes on churning out violent, mind-numbing gar-
bage that celebrates precisely those values that threaten our
existence.

It is October, 1993, and there are currently twenty-six wars
raging in the world, yet networks go on hiring "expert" psycholo-
gists to "prove" that there is no connection between the violence
and sexual obsession on our screens and the epidemics of rape
and child abuse sweeping our civilization.

The rhetoric of democracy prevents us from acknowledging our
imprisonment. We talk about a new world order while selling
lethal arms to countries who threaten it. We talk about freedom
and live in a slavery to consumerism and a worldwide celebra-

tion of just those qualities of egoism—aggression, greed, competitiveness—that keep us in Milton's great description of Satan, "Thyself not free, but to thyself enthralled," and so un-free in every sacred sense. We struggle to improve our well-being with every available ruse and pill and gadget and only succeed in straying more and more desperately from that inner sanity and peace of soul that are the only abiding sources of either physical or mental health. Anyone who tries to tell us these truths is immediately marginalized and treated as crazy or irrational or "morbidly apocalyptic."

James Baldwin, whom I revere as a writer and prophet of our culture, said to me once, "The bomb has already gone off."

"What bomb?" I asked.

"The psychic bomb, the master bomb. It goes off and nobody notices. It destroys hearts, souls and minds, while leaving the bodies and refrigerators intact."

MM: *You're painting a terrible, desperate picture. What does all of this have to do with mysticism?*

AH: Everything. George Eliot said, "The highest election known to man is to live without opium." A person with serious cancer has no chance whatever of healing if she goes on pretending she has pneumonia or a migraine. We do not have the time *not* to face what we are living in: a concentration camp of reason, where we are lied to about everything important, starting with our essential Divine identity, and where we are policed by nihilism and depression, systematically reduced to addicts of sex, money, power and status, whose incessant stimulation fuels the very system that imprisons and paralyzes us.

As the great Tibetan master Sogyal Rinpoche has written so movingly: "Sometimes I think that the greatest achievement of modern culture is its brilliant selling of samsara (of ignorance and illusion), and its barren distractions. Modern society seems to me a celebration of all the things that lead away from the truth, make truth hard to live for, and discourage people from even believing that it exists."

He continues: "This modern samsara feeds off an anxiety and depression that it carefully nurtures with a consumer machine that needs to keep us greedy to keep going. [This] samsara is highly organized, versatile and sophisticated: it assaults us from every angle with its propaganda, and creates an almost impregnable environment of addiction around us....Obsessed with hopes, dreams and ambitions which promise happiness but lead only to misery, we are like people crawling through an endless desert, dying of thirst, and all that this culture holds out to us to drink is a cup of salt water, designed to make us thirstier."

This is the clearest and most ruthless description I can offer of the concentration camp in which we currently exist.

MM: *It's a camp without walls, a camp of the mind that encourages us to become our own torturers.*

AH: And encourages us to feel worthless. This is why more of us don't escape. How did a hundred guards in Auschwitz keep thousands of prisoners docile except by making them feel disgusting, subhuman? By banning the awareness of our transcendent nature, and of spiritual wisdom in general, our culture deprives us of our true selves. We are encouraged to view ourselves as dying, greedy animals. By killing God, in the Nietzschean sense, we have come close to killing ourselves. The

Taittirya Upaniṣad tells us: "Who denies God, denies himself."
By deriding mystical truth, we have nearly severed ourselves
from any source of divine wisdom. We no longer know who we
really are and who we can be.

MM: *Rather than helping, science has added a great deal to this confusion.*

AH: Think of what the materialist scientists, high priests of this camp
who dominate biology and physics, are telling us about our
"real" nature. Stephen Jay Gould describes evolution as "a
stately dance to nowhere." Dawkins in *The Selfish Gene* informs us
that "We are survival machines, robots blindly programmed to
preserve the selfish molecules known as genes." Our interna-
tionally canonized pope of cosmic knowledge, Stephen Hawking,
pronounces, "We are insignificant creatures on a minor planet of
a very average star in the outer suburbs of one of a hundred
million galaxies…so it is difficult to believe in a God that would
care about us or even notice our existence." As if the Divine
obeys any of our categories of space, time or scale and is not as
miraculously present in a flower—as Blake and Shantideva and
Rumi and Lao Tzu have all in different ways and at different
times told us—as in the whole universe! The prestigious so-
called wisdom of our leading scientists is stunted morbid
depressiveness camouflaging itself as "empirical truth" and
"illusionless accuracy." Its false authority, completely divorced
from the essential evidence of the enlightened mind, rots our
resolve at the very moment when we need it most and deepens
that sense of impotence and worthlessness with which we are
already afflicted (as refugees from two thousand years of
Christian propaganda about "original sin"). And when you add to
this the smart relativism of the reigning contemporary philosophies—and a celebration of works with titles as absurd as
Consciousness Explained—and the neurotic conviction of our

limitations which permeates much of "serious" modern art, you come to see humanity dazed and baffled and hemmed in from all sides by images of ineptitude and meaninglessness at a moment when vision is as imperative as oxygen.

The real war in the modern world is not between democracy and communism or between capitalism and totalitarianism or between liberalism and fascism. It is the war for the mind and heart of humankind between two completely different versions of reality: the version that materialist science, most contemporary philosophy and most modern art gives human beings, as driven, dying animals in a random universe (a version that many institutionalized religions—especially Christianity and Islam—unconsciously abet with their emphasis on human sinfulness and smallness) and that version of humankind's essential, divine destiny that mystics in all ages, all spiritual traditions, all historical circumstances, have discovered and struggled to keep alive. This latter version can be summed up in the wonderful words of the great Sufi master Al Ghazzali: "Know, O Beloved, Man was not created in jest or at random, but marvelously made for some great end," or in the glorious promise of St. Francis of Assisi, "It is in dying to self that we are born to eternal life," or in the call to transcendence of the central Hindu scripture, the Bhagavad Gita, "He is forever free who has broken out of the ego cage of I and mine to be united with the lord of Love." This view can also be seen in an account by Buddhist master Nyoshul Kenpo of what enlightenment is like: "An effortless compassion can arise for all beings who have not realized their true nature. So limitless is it that if tears could express it, you would cry without end. You are naturally liberated from all suffering and fear. Then if you were to speak of the joy and bliss that arise from this realization, it is said by the Buddhas that if you were to gather all the glory, enjoyment, pleasure, and happiness of the world and put it together, it would not approach one tiny fraction of the bliss that you experience upon realizing the nature of mind."

MM: *The truth is that without an incontestable experience of transcendence—a direct perception of the sacredness of life—no sane person would care if a species capable of such atrocities survived or not.*

AH: No. And if we do not awaken to our sacred, interdependent nature, we will not know that when we allow the rain forest to burn, it is as if we were burning our own lungs, that when we pollute the seas with nuclear waste, we are lacing our own veins with poison, and that when we refuse to stop the torture in prisons all over the world or to intervene in Bosnia or to feed the starving in Asia and Africa, we are torturing, killing and starving ourselves—not figuratively, not poetically, but *literally*. When Teilhard speaks of the choice between suicide and adoration, he is not referring to some gorgeous kind of emotionalism but to the highest means of opening to the sacred truths of reality in order to arm ourselves with the love and clarity that will protect our world.

MM: *Our prevailing image of God in the West as a judgmental entity separate from ourselves will have to be transcended for this wisdom you're discussing to take hold.*

AH: A secular culture does not teach that God is power absolutely informed with love. Love is the transforming and creative power of the universe. Any power that is not love is not real power. The West has simply not been able to understand that it is divine wisdom and goodness that irradiate true intelligence, not the intellect. Our inability to understand that traps us in our present nihilism.

How else would the ego interpret God except as a greater monster than itself? It cannot see God completely as love because if it did, it would fall in love with the love and want to enter it. That great love would burn the camp walls down with peace and destroy the prison. The ego cannot afford to understand the nature of God as love because if it did, it would die of heartbreak and longing.

The ego can only go on surviving when it sees God as its own projection, as Hitler writ large. The fantasy that the ego has created of existence—that there's only death here—necessitates a sadistic God who's created this terminal theater.

MM: *God is our ideal torturer, then, the abusive father without a heart.*

AH: We've grown up in the shadow of a debased Christianity that gloats over our failings without teaching us what Matthew Fox calls "original blessing." The Christian Church has, for many centuries, given up its vital responsibility to create living mystics of great attainment. It has concentrated on the external without doing the essential work of transformation. What I hope the Christian Church will learn from the great explosion of mystical understanding that is sweeping the West is to take very seriously the Buddhist and Hindu technologies of sacredness and create its own circle of masters who have been Christed, who can lead not with words, but from full realization. Just imagine if a great contemporary Catholic saint had the courage that St. Francis had to get up and say, "This Church is rotten at its core. It is destroying the energy of Christ in the world, making it impossible for this glorious power to heal the world at the moment it needs it most." I have a fantasy about Mother Teresa getting up at one of these endless Vatican councils and telling the Church that it must give all its money to the poor, embrace the sick and homosexuals and women, stop abetting monstrous regimes all over the world and put into practice Christ's injunctions to end the reign of injustice on the earth. Think what a revolution that might bring!

Imagine too if the Church could take seriously what the Virgin is saying in Medjugorje. What is a Church worth that cannot stand behind divine revelation? Which cannot say yes to its direct mediatrix at a crucial moment in world history who is saying absolutely essential things before millions of believers every day? The creation is groaning for the Divine Mother today, but her message of universal tolerance and the abandonment of dogma is too threatening for the hierarchy to absorb.

Christ is *longing* to come to the center of the world's mind in an authentic way, to play his part in the transformation. Although the crucifixion and resurrection are of course inseparable, I think the emphasis on a risen, glorified Christ should prevail at this moment. This would give Christianity a version of Christ in his final, mystical splendor and help Christians worship the potential of the enlightened, resurrected One in all of us. It would encourage Christians to view the whole universe as tending toward a transfiguration in the light, what Teilhard called the "omega point." This would link Christianity directly with the ancient Eastern traditions of enlightenment and pave the way forward for all the mystical traditions to work in harmony together towards the same goal of a transformed humanity.

MM: *What use are the so-called New Age philosophies in this necessary transformation?*

AH: That is a complex question. The New Age is a grab bag of many different unrelated pieces of various traditions and fantasy, and while it has undoubtedly helped many to begin a spiritual path, it has many of the marks of the diseases it is pretending to cure.

It is hardly surprising that a materialist culture without a wisdom tradition and, until recently, almost completely ignorant of the laws of inner change, would spawn the kind of consumerist, naive and narcissistic spirituality we see all around us.

This would be less dangerous if the stakes were not so high. What lies before us is so demanding that only a sober, unsparing, mature vision of what transformation entails can be of use to us now, a vision that does not lie to us about the sacrifice or the difficulty or the darkness. So many of the visions on sale are palliatives, placebos, half-truths that misrepresent the rigorous nature of spiritual life and the necessity to work with an authentic master.

As in the Christian Church, there are very few realized mystics working as teachers in the New Age. Almost anyone can set up shop, and desperation will always provide customers. In an age that adores instant solutions, there is a hungry audience for versions of the journey that offer instant enlightenment for a few dollars. In an age that adores ease and castrates us with comfort, it is not surprising that pop philosophy should promise sudden divine shifts that will save us all (and floatings off to other planets in spaceships). These are some of the "Camp's" most insidious lies, since they masquerade as escapes from it.

MM: *There's a dangerous confusion in the New Age between absolute and relative reality as defined by the perennial traditions. Ramana Maharshi says that "Brahman is real...the universe is unreal, and that Brahman is the universe. The third statement explains the first two; it signifies that when the universe is perceived apart from Brahman, that perception is false and*

illusory." Unfortunately, people misunderstand this subtle point to mean
that matter doesn't matter, that only the transcendent is of value. This
confusion drains us of responsibility and outrage.

AH: The Divine exists. Humankind is being helped. There are realized
masters on the earth. However, it is essential that we not be
distracted from the real task ahead by a misunderstanding of the
laws of absolute reality, or spiritual diversion. The light can save
us, but we must work with it.

MM: *We need, in point of fact, a clear "science" of enlightenment, stripped of New*
Age vagueness and naiveté.

AH: Yes, desperately. If we had only the external sciences to rely on,
the game would already be lost. Fortunately, there exists
another empiricism altogether, interrelated technologies of
spiritual transformation developed by all the major mystical
traditions and still, miraculously, intact and available to us. It is
time that Westerners realize that mystics are scientists in their
domain, that mystical union and transformation obey laws as
inexorable as those of the physical universe. These laws are
documented by systems of the most sublime sophistication
which can help us take the journey into truth.

Vedanta is such a system, so are Sufism, Kabbala, Taoism,
Theravada and Mahayana Buddhism, and the disciplines of such
highly evolved cultures as the Kogis and the Aborigines. So is
the system that could be developed in the Christian tradition
from the meditation techniques of the Desert Fathers and the
writings of, among others, Ruysbroeck, Eckhart, Teresa of Avila,
Hildegard of Bingen and St. John of the Cross. These technologies have in common the knowledge that the Divine Self is the
one essential fact of the cosmos, and ways to reveal and realize

it are known and have been charted. Maps of the most helpful accuracy exist and can be interpreted with the help of those who have taken the journey. Astonishing similarities in the laws that each of these great systems honor—laws of meditation and contemplation, faith and devotion, clarity, resignation, surrender and adoration—prove their legitimacy.

These are the laws of the only science that can reveal to us the essence of what we are and the essence of reality. If these laws are not now widely known and respected and acted on, it seems obvious now that the human adventure will soon end.

Part Two

2

THE MYSTIC DILEMMA

The real problem behind these many controversies was the fact that no language existed in which one could speak consistently about the new situation. The ordinary language is based upon the old concepts of space and time.

—Werner Heisenberg

Suppose a man has seen the ocean and somebody asks him, "Well, what is the ocean like?" The first man opens his mouth as wide as he can and says, "What a sight! What tremendous waves and sounds!"

—Ramakrishna

This is where words fail, for it is not of the past, present, or future.

—Third Zen Patriarch

MM: *Unfortunately, mystics throughout history have frequently been accused of excess, exaggeration, hallucination—even outright fakery. In times like these that favor minimalism and cold, hard facts, this breach between the mystic mind and the prevailing rationalism has grown almost unbridgeable.*

AH: It's crucial to address at the outset of these talks the problem of mystical language, what might be called its excessive, extravagant, theatrical side. The Upanishads talk of the ultimate samadhi being the bursting of a thousand suns. Rumi talks about the hundred suns in the heart of the Beloved that make all the hearts of the world burn. The Sufi master Shabestari says, "Know that the world...is a mirror. In each atom nests a hundred flaming suns. From the split heart of one sole drop of water emerge a hundred pure oceans..."

It is easy to dismiss this kind of language as exaggeration, hysterical folly. It's easy to see the almost insane enthusiasm that the real mystic can manifest in moments as a form of psychosis. It's not surprising that throughout history, mystics have been tortured, burnt, humiliated, derided, because what they reveal to the ego is the dreariness of its joys, the desolation of its empire, the vast dullness of its understanding. The ego's revenge for being told the shattering good news that would end its dominion is to make the mystic look absurd.

Simone Weil said about the *Song of Songs*, "It is hardly surprising that the mystics who wrote this should use the language of passion. Other kinds of lovers only borrow the language of passion but it is the mystic's by right."

What we hear in Josquin des Prez's music and in stretches of Beethoven's *Missa Solemnis* and in the poetry of Rumi, Kabir, Vyasa, Rabia, Mirabai is a passion that makes all forms of worldly passion look absurdly tame; an intensity that makes all forms of worldly intensity look barren; a wildness that makes all forms of worldly wildness look crippled.

There is no exaggeration in the language of the Upanishads and other mystic technologies. Actually, they underplay the experience. Language cannot express the extremity of the explosion of gnosis. It will never be able to; language ends where gnosis begins. What can language do? It can throw out its arms and dance. It can fling all its jewels at the Beloved's feet. It can create a Taj Mahal in words, ransacking the world of the imagination for all its most priceless things, just as Shah Jahan ransacked the world for chryselephantine and emeralds and rubies and seed pearls and Burmese teak. Just as Shah Jahan knew that creating that most amazing of buildings would be always only a pale shadow of the beauty of his wife and of the imageless splendor of his adoration of her, so the mystic knows that whatever he or she creates out of this great love will fall a million miles short of it. Their courage is to go on speaking of the unspeakable.

MM: *Or else?*

AH: To remain completely silent, as many masters have done. Otherwise, there is no alternative but to use all the resources of language and art of every kind to begin to express something of the splendor of truth, so that people trapped in illusion can begin to capture some part of the glory that is our true inheritance. It could not be a more difficult and discouraging time in which to do work like this. This time, as Kierkegaard and Nietzsche pointed out, institutionalizes the discouragement of passion, makes every effort to anesthetize it and deride it. Kierkegaard said that living in industrial culture was like being trampled to death by geese. If he could say that in the 1830s, what would he say about what it is like to be alive today? In the *Mathnawi*, Rumi asks us to imagine what it would be like to tell an embryo in the womb about the world outside, the grasses, the birds, the marriage feasts, the dances, spiritual love. What would the embryo say? It would say: "The world you are describing does not exist. All that exists is this dark place I am in."

At any other time, mystics could find excuses to keep silent; we

could vanish or live our own private lives. Most mystic technologies—the Sufi, the Tibetan, the Hindu, the Christian—kept many
of the secrets away from people. They knew that the secrets
could only be understood by actual experience. But we now live
in a time far too dangerous for that kind of silence. If the news of
the true identity of human beings does not get out in the most
striking way possible, the very future of the world is in jeopardy.
We cannot afford that withdrawal; yet to talk nakedly as a mystic
today is to risk everything.

MM: *These problems of mystic testimony are little known in the West. Mystics
have the tremendous difficulty of trying to communicate the truth of truths to
a world which doesn't believe that truth is possible, in which most people in
the media are metropolitan skeptics of a very tough kind.*

AH: I would like to send them all this quotation from Simone Weil
on a postcard, "Men [or women] of the most brilliant intelligence can be born, live, and die in error and falsehood. In them
intelligence is neither good, nor even an asset. The difference
between more or less intelligent men is like the difference
between criminals condemned to life imprisonment in smaller
and larger cells. The intelligent person who is proud of his or her
intelligence is like a condemned person proud of his or her cell."

This reminds me of a story I love that the Tibetan Master Patrul
Rinpoche used to tell. There was a frog that lived in a dank dark
well. You might call that well New York or Paris or London or
any of the urban prisons of the mind in which most of us live.
The frog thought that the whole world was this dank well. One
day another frog came to visit him from the sea. The two of them
sat rather disconsolately on one of the mossy stones in the dank
well. The well frog asked, "Where do you come from?"

"I come from the sea."

"What is the sea like? How big is it?"

"The sea is enormous."

"Oh, you mean about a quarter of the size of this well."

At that the frog from the sea clutched his sides and started to laugh outrageously. The laughter grew, and tears ran down his cheeks. The well frog said, "Well, what do you mean? It's about half the size of the well, as big as that?"

The sea frog laughed more, finally dried his eyes and said, "Honestly, I promise you, you know nothing. You know less than nothing if you imagine that the sea could be contained in any way in this well. The sea stretches from one end of the world to another; it cannot be described but you can see it. I will take you if you want to see it."

The frog from the well was amazed by the fervor of the sea frog, and he made the choice at that moment to go on a journey to the sea. It led through all the different valleys described by Attar in the "Conference of the Birds," the valley of love, bewilderment, loss and abandonment. One day when the frog from the well was pretty worn out, the frog from the sea took him to a hill, told him to close his eyes, walk up the steps. The sea frog said, "Now open your eyes."

The frog from the well opened his eyes and saw the vast luminous sea. At that moment his head exploded in a thousand pieces.

Our civilization is almost entirely made up of well frogs who live in a pit of rationalism. We've been told again and again that all visions of the sea, whether Christian or Buddhist or Sufi, are infantile rubbish or fantasy or the opiate of the masses. But the frogs from the sea are amongst us, and the bridges of reason are burning in front of our eyes. And what is being born in the hearts and open minds of people all over the world at this tragic moment is something marvelous and completely fresh that cannot be contained, limited or explained by any of the words or dogmas or patterns of the past.

3

STRADDLING EAST AND WEST

AH: The possibility and leap of understanding that is being described in the frog story is comparable to explaining the Eastern
understanding of the Divine Self to a Westerner not open to it.

MM: *You know this challenge of straddling East and West from first-hand
experience. Your life and writing have been equally rooted in Western and
Eastern cultures. As a hybrid of both hemispheres, how do you view the
difference between Western and Eastern egos and their distinct approaches to
spirituality?*

AH: I've talked with several masters who work all over the world, and
they tell me that they find advantages and drawbacks to both.
Easterners have a natural piety and natural devotion, but they
don't work very hard. A Tibetan master told me once about
going back to Tibet. Hundreds of people came to bring him
presents but didn't stay to listen to his dharma talk; they wanted
a blessing and nothing more. The same master said that if, on
the other hand, you can get Westerners to do spiritual work, they
will do it with ardor and passion. If you can persuade Westerners
that enlightenment exists, they will pursue it with a sophistication that is difficult for Easterners to match.

Once Westerners decide to pursue the spiritual life, they do so
from a position of having exhausted a great deal of material

temptation—many of the various sexual, emotional and material illusions that an extremely resourceful samsara can give to
them. In a certain way, Westerners who have "easternized" their
hearts and souls may be the most sophisticated beings that
have ever been produced on the earth. They have developed all
sorts of skills of discrimination that can then be very useful in
the movement toward God. The Easterners' natural piety can
stop them from needing to explore further. There are many
ironies at play.

MM: *So much has been said about the deficiencies of the Western spirit that it's*
refreshing to hear about the benefits of being born here.

AH: I've been harsh on the West and on what I've called the concentration camp of reason, but there is another way of looking at
our contemporary disaster. The very extent of the West's sickness can also be used as a road to health. A Westerner can see
the devastating cost of the false self very clearly. To acknowledge
that is to awaken from a whole illusion of progress, to use that
energy to end this destruction and to establish sacred technologies which could give humankind unprecedented kinds of power.
It's almost as if samsara in the Western form had been allowed
to develop so that we could acquire certain skills in separation
from nature and God which we could never have acquired in
unity. For example, we might never have gone so far in scientific
exploration if we had been content to rest in a nondual state. A
fall may have been necessary for this amazing explosion of
knowledge to take place. The emphasis on material things has
meant an attention to the body, to the creation, to the external
world which ancient philosophies sometimes ignored. There
have been great advances in medicine, technology and political
rights which have been won and must not be given up. Also, the
Western passion for justice and democracy, married to the

sacred lesson of the East, could create a new world order. The Dalai Lama has admitted that Tibet made a mistake in ignoring the world for the total pursuit of enlightenment, in not understanding Chinese foreign policy and in not defending itself by joining the League of Nations and the international community which could, perhaps, have protected it.

Many Westerners are waking up to the dangers of Western power, and this gives their search a particular intensity. It isn't just because the West is so sick that so many masters live here now. It is also because the energy of awakening is so vibrant and inventive here.

MM: *This integration suggests a new position entirely for the future—a third position which joins the strengths of East and West, heals the division between spirit and matter, heart and mind and unifies humankind. Aspiring toward this third position is crucial.*

AH: Without question. I think we are coming into the age of the global mind in a far larger sense than Marshall McLuhan ever imagined. It is as if the West and East are two sides of the essential mind of humanity. The East has developed to its furthest point the love and understanding of the transcendent. The West in the heroic struggle of the last four hundred years has come to an unprecedented awareness of the laws governing the nature of matter. But because both developed out of touch with the other, both are radically imbalanced.

India has given us the most sublime spirituality that the world has known, but this gift has not helped her deal with the injustice of the caste system or heal the wounds of poverty. The West has learned how to go to the moon but forgotten its own soul. What is needed is to bring together in harmony and mutual respect the two severed sides of the global mind. Technology and the availability in translation of all the major texts of the various mystical traditions is making this possible for the first time. It is this synthesis that will provide the spiritual energy and technical knowledge for the work of transformation that awaits us.

MM: *A master mind of that transformation was, of course, Sri Aurobindo.*

AH: Yes. He was a great prophet of this synthesis—an Indian who was educated in England and had an extraordinary command of Western culture. Meeting Aurobindo's work in Pondicherry when I was twenty-five transformed my life. I found in him a thinker whose majesty and scope shook me to my core. He combined the Western and Eastern mind in a revolutionary way. He had all the rigor and passion for political change of a Westerner and all the intricate awareness of metaphysical reality that the highest Hindu philosophy and the most extensive inner mystical experience could provide.

In his two great books, *The Synthesis of Yoga* and *The Life Divine*, he envisaged nothing less than the evolution of a new kind of being on earth and of a life on earth and in the body that would be lived consciously for and as the Divine. His vision transcends all categories of Eastern and Western thought and is in fact a direct emanation of the healed global mind. It is a marriage of the most refined insights of Western materialism and Eastern mysticism to create a third position beyond both, a position to which our contemporary ordeal is inviting the whole of human-kind.

"The whole of life is the Yoga of Nature," he tells us in *The Synthesis of Yoga*. "The Yoga that we seek must also be an integral action of

Nature…if indeed our aim be only an escape from the world to God, synthesis is unnecessary and a waste of time. But if our aim be a transformation of our integral being into the terms of God existence, it is then that a synthesis becomes necessary."

MM: *He wrote extensively on the importance of the Mother to this synthesis as well.*

AH: This great revolution that Aurobindo envisioned would be enacted under the aegis of the Divine Mother. Nothing in any of my reading or inner experience prepared me for what I found in his work when I first encountered it at twenty-six in Pondicherry, a vision of the Divine Mother, of God as the Mother, so radical, so potent, so all-embracing that it overturned and transformed completely everything I had hitherto understood of God. At last I found a vision of the Divine that satisfied my heart and mind and answered my profound needs for a belief in a dynamic Feminine Power that could reshape a world I experienced as deformed by patriarchal rationalism and greed; for a relationship with the Divine that would be fearless, unpuritanical and as completely tender, shameless, and intimate as the ideal relationship between mother and child.

Aurobindo convinced me that the force of boundless love, the immense creative power that is the Shakti, the Mother aspect of God, the Divine Mother, would be brought back to the center of the human psyche after thousands of years of repression mirrored in our contempt for our bodies and nature herself and provide the divine energy that can make the transformation possible. The Mother's is the consciousness and gentle, all-embracing wisdom that can heal, harmonize, balance, and integrate at the very deepest levels the two alienated sides of the human enterprise. Aurobindo showed me that if there is to be a livable future, it will without question wear the crown of feminine design.

4

THE SACRED FEMININE, THE MOTHER AND THE LIGHT

To the property of motherhood belong nature, love, wisdom and knowledge and this is God...God speaking to Julian: I it am. The greatness and goodness of the Father, I it am: The wisdom and kindness of the Mother, I it am: The light and grace that is all blessed love, I it am.

— Julian of Norwich

When you make the two one, and when you make the inner as the outer and the above as the below, and when you make the male and female into a single one, so that the male will not be male and the female not be female...then you shall enter the kingdom.

—Gospel of Thomas, Logion 22

MM: *You're saying that the whole human future depends on whether humankind can rediscover and restore the sacred feminine to the core of human awareness.*

AH: Yes. A long tragic imbalance of the masculine has brought humankind to the moment when unless it recovers the feminine powers of the psyche—of intuition, patience, reverence for nature, knowledge of the holy unity of things—and marries these powers with the masculine energies of will, reason, passion for order and control, life will end on the planet. This marriage of the masculine with the feminine has to take place in all of our hearts and minds, whether we are male or female. The mystical and practical health it brings is the goal of being human, the basis and energy of all true transformation.

The chaos and tragedy we are surrounded by makes it clear that the patriarchy has failed, that scientific rationalism and the cult of technological progress taken to fanatic lengths are suicidal and that humankind dissociated from the wisdom of nature is doomed. Everything now depends on whether we as a race can restore ourselves to sacred balance and find again that ancient, eternal, natural way of harmony, peace, adoration and reverence for being that is still walked by the Kogis, Yamomamis, American Indians and Aborigines and that underlies, permeates and subtly illumines some part of all the major religions, however far they have strayed from it. If we do not learn again our divine identity as children of the Divine Mother and Father, our interdependence with everything that lives and our responsibility for all our actions and for nature itself, we will destroy ourselves and our world.

I find it helpful to see the development of humanity in broadly three stages. The first stage was, as many archaeologists and anthropologists now agree, matriarchal. Humankind lived in real and magical harmony with nature and worshipped the goddess, the Mother, and her body, the creation, and knew life and death as two modes of one divine reality. The second stage—the patriarchal—began in the millennium before the birth of Christ with the rise of the hero myth, the shattering of the harmony of the old goddess archetypes and the development of rational inquiry in Greece. This stage saw the separation of the Creator from the creation, an increasing sense of divorce between heaven and earth and the triumph of a divisive, categorizing, dissociative kind of knowing. In this second stage, humankind left the womb of the Mother and developed extraordinary powers of manipulation and domination of nature. There was, however, an illness at the root of this enterprise. It depended for much of its energy on a denial of our fundamental connected-ness to each other and to the world and on an increasingly schizophrenic rejection of all those values—of nurture, intuition, unity, tenderness and bliss—associated with the abandoned Mother.

MM: *Nature, soul, matter, the body and its instincts, the imagination were all in the process devalued and desacralized. Would you agree that the further patriarchal consciousness moved from the Mother, the more it subconsciously feared her and derided her powers?*

AH: Yes. And this led inexorably to the creation of the worldwide concentration camp we inhabit—a camp in which nature herself and everything natural in us is in danger of being tortured to death.

MM: *That is where we are now, and many, many people are beginning to know it. Yet obviously we can't regress to that matriarchal stage again. There must be, as we've said, a new position.*

AH: I believe there is only one position we could possibly take and still survive. That is the stage of what I call the sacred marriage. This stage will have to involve the restoration to human respect of all the rejected powers of the feminine, of the Mother. But it is absolutely essential that this restoration should be accom-plished in the deep spirit of the sacred feminine—in her spirit of unconditional love, tolerance, forgiveness, all-embracing and all-harmonizing balance—and not in any sense involve a swing

in the other direction, towards a facile or furious rejection of
everything masculine or scientific or patriarchal. A restoration of
the sacred feminine that is fanatical and harsh is a contradiction
in terms and would only engender more global lunacy. It would
be, in fact, a disaster and the waste of a supreme opportunity for
healing. The last thing that is needed now is another dogma or
religion—the dogma or religion of the Mother—a creation in the
name of balance and harmony of yet another set of judgmental
and imprisoning rules and categories.

What is needed, in the hearts and minds of all of us, is for the
sacred marriage between masculine and feminine to take place
and birth humility, delight, the capacity to feel and love deeply,
humor and profound and active spiritual awareness. What is
needed to preserve the world is an extension of this inner sacred
marriage into every domain and activity—a marriage, at the
most fundamental level then, between yin and yang, science and
mysticism, prayer and service, wisdom and politics. This sacred
marriage would restore to the world that vision it desperately
needs—of the unity of all things. And it is this vision that the
Mother in her various incarnations on the earth and all the
genuine mystical masters, male or female, are trying to birth in
the world. We are being brought as a race by destiny and our
own terrible mistakes to a moment in which we will have to
choose the maturity of the sacred marriage and the all-encom-
passing knowledge of unity it brings, will have to open to the
feminine wisdom of humility and mystery, to have a future at all.
But what a transformed future it could be if we did!

MM: *Will you try now to define more closely the wisdom of the sacred feminine?*

AH: The sacred feminine is very hard to define because her essence
         is subtlety, flexibility and mystery, and her essential work the

radiant overcoming of the definitions of the mind by love and immediate knowledge of the interdependence of all things, all being. But I think the wisdom of the sacred feminine has three fundamental powers, all of which, naturally, interrelate and interpenetrate. The first is a knowledge of the unity of all life, the simple naked knowledge that all life is one. Scientists are now discovering what the most ancient tribes have always known— that everything is connected in an infinite web and that in the making of one blade of grass or rabbit or tree or human being, the whole universe takes part. Instinctual to this knowledge of unity are respect, reverence, adoration, natural gratitude and natural compassion for all animate and inanimate, visible and invisible beings. Extending this ancient knowledge of unity of the sacred feminine to an embrace of all religious paths, all mystical traditions, was the marvelous achievement of Ramakrishna. The Mother, he tells us, cooks the white fish of awareness in different ways depending on the appetite and taste of her children. Some like it with strips of mango; some like it curried, some plain. But everyone is still eating the same fish. Restoration of the sacred feminine would mean the end of all quarrels between the religions—not an end of the differences— why shouldn't the different ways of cooking the fish go on?—but an end forever of any one path's claim to exclusive truth. In the wisdom of the sacred feminine, life is one. All paths lead to the one. We are all the children of God, the Father-Mother, sitting down together at the divine feast of life, each eating its food in his or her own unique way but dependent on the same light source.

MM: *And the second power of the sacred feminine?*

AH: I have come to know it most simply as rhythm, the law of rhythm. The sacred feminine awakens us to the knowledge that the universe has its own laws and harmonies which are already whole, already perfect, and which, if we are to live wisely, we have to intuit, revere and follow. These laws are essentially rhythmic—as the seasons are rhythmic, as the relation between masculine and feminine in the psyche and the forces of nature is rhythmic—and opening to these laws and learning to honor and enact them necessitates our developing feminine powers of intuition, attention, receptivity, capacity to wonder and nurture and cherish, and a musical flexibility of approach that tries to mirror the astonishing suppleness of life itself and its myriad changes. This awareness of the rhythms of the universe and of life is simply not accessible to the masculine powers of reason and will on their own. They are blinded by their impatient desire to know definitively, to manipulate, to control. But the feminine, lunar side of the psyche is aware of the rhythms of life quite naturally and spontaneously accepts and welcomes guidance. If we wish to heal the natural world that we are in danger of destroying, we are going to have to listen in humility to its voices and attend faithfully to its rhythms. This listening and this attention are essential to our survival and are the gifts of the sacred feminine, the Mother.

The third power of the sacred feminine springs out of the other two. For myself, I call it the love of the dance. In this love, life itself, in all its paradoxes, is seen as completely sacred, to be adored and honored in all its ordeals and wonders. Life is the mystery of the Father-Mother, to be worshipped as their play of love, the ecstatic dance of their presence. This is a fundamentally unmorbid, healthy, joyful vision of the world, one that blesses and accepts it bravely in its entirety, one that honors the body and sexuality and does not deny them, that reveres the family and all forms of what Keats called the "holiness of the heart's affections," that sees and knows matter and nature as the body of the Divine Mother, the body of the light. The wisdom of the sacred feminine is one that knows—beyond all concepts or dogmas—that this experience, this process of life we are all in— is holy in its minutest detail and that so-called ordinary life is not ordinary at all, but one unbroken flow of normal miracle. This sacred wisdom does not separate heaven from earth, spirit from body, prayer from action. For it, all dimensions, all worlds, all possibilities, are here, are interrelated, are one. This is a wisdom that does not aim for an unnatural perfection or a flight into some life or body-denying absolute—but works patiently, all-embracingly, with infinite alchemical subtlety towards wholeness, a wholeness in which the transcendent and mystical are not separated from the immanent and practical but married with them. For those awakened by and to this wisdom, being born a human being is not being born into a fallen desolate world of sin or mere illusion; to be human is to be born into a dance that every animate or inanimate, visible or invisible being is also dancing, a dance whose every step is printed in light, whose energy is adoration and whose rhythm is praise. Pain, desolation and destruction are not separate from this dance but essential energies of its transformative unfolding. And death itself cannot shatter the dance, because death is the life-spring of its fertility, the mother of all its changing splendor.

MM: *How far this vision is from the one the major religions give us!*

AH: I think we have to face the fact that all the major religions without exception have failed us. They belong to the second, largely patriarchal stage of human development I have been proposing and, so, partake in varying degrees of that stage's dissociativeness and schizophrenia. If their wisdom had been powerful and inspiring and all-embracing enough, we would not be in the disaster we are now, and the madness of an exaggerated rationalism and a virtually demonic worship of technology could never have so seduced and devastated the human psyche. What has deformed all of the major religions as they have developed historically is a dangerous over-emphasis on transcendence. This could hardly be otherwise because, with the dismemberment of the matriarchy, came a nailing down of the power of women in all cultures and a consequent rejection of the values of natural process associated with women, nature, bodies, birth, rhythm, all the holy radiance of life itself. The Creator was removed from creation and creation abandoned to the will of the masculine which is increasingly divorced from the balancing power of the feminine. This fear of women and bodies and matter is in all the major religions, even, subtly, in some kinds of Hinduism and in Mahayana Buddhism.

MM: *And these fears are linked to an exaggerated lust for transcendence?*

AH: Yes. This complex nexus of fears, anxieties, repressions and evasions has fundamentally limited all the major religions, although in each of their core revelations and mystical traditions there are glowing traces of the wisdom of the sacred feminine which cannot completely be covered over. But the depth of the denial of the feminine and so of nature, matter and the holiness of the process of life itself, is shattering, extreme and hard to face in all of its unnerving interconnections. When you see just how extensive it is and how this denial penetrates and warps the highest mystical metaphysics, even, of the greatest religions, it leaves one aghast and deeply shaken by the human power of rejection and amnesia. But we all must now let ourselves be aghast in this way, because until each one of us in every aspect of our inner and outer lives has become aware of the impact of this denial of the feminine, no real change in our image of the Divine is possible, and the restoration of balance and the sacred marriage cannot take place. This is a vast, often dismaying work, but it must be done.

MM: *Do you see Christianity as the principal villain in this denial?*

AH: In a way. Certainly the villain is not the Christianity of Christ but the official historical Christianity we have come to know, with its obsession with original sin and the falleness of the body, human nature and nature itself. This dreadful vision has been a disaster for the human race. Christ's knowledge of the glory of being and the sacredness of all things has been denied or distorted, with the result that we Westerners have not in any way been restrained by the Church and its spiritual philosophy from exploiting and nearly destroying nature. In fact the Church's vision of nature as fallen has unconsciously abetted the exploitation of the natural world. What was there to stop Westerners from trying madly to subject all of reality to their will, when the traditional Christian way of reading the creation chapter of Genesis stressed human dominion over nature, at the expense of any sacred responsibility? As for the doctrine of original sin as developed by the Church, it has fundamentally unnerved and repressed us in a way that has fuelled and not in any way checked human destructiveness and has exacerbated that fear, desolation, inability to trust and sense of separation from God that is at the core of all destructiveness. What is there to cherish or save if this life is rotten at its core with sin and what possible use would there be in striving for divine wholeness in the dance if sin is always bound to fetter up our feet?

What is sobering, however, is that this tragic and dangerous rejection of life and matter is not the province of Christianity alone. All the major religions are scarred by it. Official Islam is patriarchal, woman and body-hating and fanatical to a terrifying degree. Most schools of Judaism view the Creator as absolutely transcendent of the creation and men as the exclusive vessels of sacred transmission. While Hinduism and Buddhism have, in my opinion, by far the subtlest and richest vision of the psyche and of the Divine and have preserved their great mystical traditions, there are dangers inherent in both of their philosophies, as their historical development has shown.

As Aurobindo pointed out so trenchantly throughout his work, the sacred life-consecrating and life-celebrating wisdom of an earlier Hindu vision—that enshrined in the Vedas and the Gita—was historically overtaken and weakened by a one-sided view of the world as *maya* or illusion, with consequences that enervated a whole civilization. The life-denying, body-denying, antifeminine tendencies of both traditional Theravada and to a lesser extent, traditional Mahayana Buddhism are also extremely disturbing. In many schools of Thai Theravada Buddhism, one cannot attain enlightenment in a woman's body. The most a woman can do is serve the monks. Very early on in the development of Buddhism, male monks separated from society and were seen as superior to it. The entire purpose of incarnation was seen as liberation from samsara. There is an extremism, fear of nature, and repressed hysteria in this which Mahayana Buddhism—especially in its wonderful vision of divine service in the ideal of the bodhisattva—tried to correct. But even in the Mahayana women are still drastically undervalued (the Tibetan word for woman means "lesser birth") and the heroic emphasis on enlightenment can lead to a separation from this life and its active responsibilities and a radical undervaluing of the sacred wisdom of ordinary life. How many practicing and serious Western Hindus and Buddhists have told me that it does not really matter if the world is destroyed, because this dimension is only maya, only illusion. This is not sacred wisdom; it is folly and escapism.

MM: *So what you are saying is that the major religions have in a way, however unconsciously, conspired in the destruction we are now enduring?*

AH: Because they lost fundamental contact with the sacred feminine and its knowledge of unity, rhythm and dance and because they repressed women who partly guard that knowledge, the major religions were unable to give humankind a complete enough inspiration to prevent the destruction of nature, and this is still the case. This does not mean that the major religions should be scrapped but that each of their revelations has to be subjected to scrutiny. Anything that does not help humankind into the most invigorating and inspiring possible vision of its sacred identity and purpose and of the total holiness of nature has to be set outside. To save ourselves at this late moment, we have to believe passionately in our deepest selves, in God's uncondi-tional love for us and in our worth. To struggle and sacrifice to save nature, we have to believe, see and know nature in its divine splendor and know that we and nature are one—one dance, one feast, one radiance whose beauty and joy it would be madness not to do everything in our power to preserve.

Each major religion will have to, I believe, go through two connected revolutions to be useful in the transformation, both of which will cost great suffering and entail great courage. The first revolution is a mystical one—a return to the mystical revelation at the core of the religion and a stripping away of all divisive or fanatical trappings. The second revolution is in many ways even more radical. This revolution would entail the open-ing of this mystical core not only to the revelations of all other mystical traditions in a spirit of passionate and authentic dialogue but, more importantly still, to the wisdom of the sacred

feminine. Each of the mystical traditions separately and together, has to, I believe, let the divine feminine consciously
and completely into its core so that the Mother can heal, refine,
purify, harmonize and embolden them all and make them
practical in this great ordeal. In each of the mystical traditions,
the sacred feminine is already partially present. There can be
no real mysticism without profound feminine receptivity. But
now the Mother, in all of them, must be present in her fullness
and glory so that, at the heart of each of them, the sacred
marriage can take place and each of them can become practical
training-grounds for servants of peace and unity. This is an
immense demand, I know, but if the world religions do not go
through these revolutions and this tuning by the divine feminine, they will continue to be part of the problem and not the
solution to it.

MM: *Couldn't a great deal of this tuning of the sacred feminine in the major
religions come from a greater openness to the native traditions and to the
religions of indigenous tribes? Isn't it in them that we see most clearly now
the wisdom of the way, of the great balance?*

AH: I would go so far as to say that if we do not listen with respect
and humility to what the Kogis, Native Americans, Bushmen,
Ladakhis and Aborigines have to tell us, we will not survive.
They have everything to teach us about the interrelatedness
of things in nature and the honoring of nature. Many of the
indigenous tribes—the Kogis, Aborigines, Native Americans in
particular—have very developed, powerful and precise prophetic
traditions that could be of enormous help to us if we let them.
These prophetic traditions arise out of a relationship with the
world and with nature at once more visionary and more rooted
than ours, and they warn us with a passion, an urgency, a dignity
and a quite extraordinary accuracy of what will happen if we

continue to disobey in a way that none of the major religions can muster. This should not surprise us. The tribes of the earth love and honor the earth and know her as their Mother; they are not drugged on power or hierarchy or some desperate dream of transcendence. Because of what most of them have suffered at our hands and at the hands of our vision of progress, the tribal peoples of the world are far more awake than we are to the facts of our hubris and its cost—without any technological or religious consolation. In each of their prophetic traditions is a different voice of the Mother trying to reach, guide, inspire, warn and heal us. We must abandon all technological or religious pride and listen with our whole being.

I have recently read Robert Lawlor's *Voices of the First Day*, an illumined account of the living vision of the Aborigines. It was a humbling experience. I saw very clearly how much I and all of us in the modern world have to learn and how the vision of the Aborigines in its brilliance, subtlety and completeness is as worthy of our reverence as the highest mysticism of the major religions. Their vision may be even more priceless to us now, springing as it does from the heart of a people that never lost or betrayed the divine feminine, or even imagined doing so. We cannot go back to the nonagrarian gatherer world of the Aborigines, but we can learn from the incandescence of their total trust of nature and life. Without their kind of wisdom, in fact, we cannot go forward. This wisdom is echoed, with countless inspired variations, in the philosophies and practices of many tribes around the world who are anxious to share what they know with us to help us save ourselves and them. We must, we have to, listen. The pure, fierce, illusionless intensity of their warnings is, for me, a proof of their authenticity. These warnings are the earth's last wake-up call to us.

MM: *Inherent in everything you are saying is a vision of the Divine Mother. Who or what is She, exactly?*

AH: No definitions of the Mother could ever be adequate. The Mother is beyond all dogmas, all definitions, all qualifications of any kind. One of the questions I kept asking Bede Griffiths in our final conversations as he was dying was "What is the Mother to you now?" He would smile and always say, "There are no words for her."

Having said that, I will risk saying something that I hope is not too limiting or too foolish. The experience of the Mother, of the Mother-aspect of the Godhead, of the Motherhood of God, is an immense, vast, constantly expanding experience of the presence of calm and blissful unconditional love as the ground of all being. Everything is in the Mother, everything is the Mother and the Mother is beyond everything, constantly drawing everything deeper and deeper into the fire of her always transforming love. She is at once the ground, the energy and the always changing and flowering goal of evolution, the spider that spins the great cosmic web and lives in it, the web itself and the dark luminous womb and void out of which both spider and web are constantly being born.

The truth of so immense and paradoxical a definition—if what I have said can be called a definition—can never be understood by the mind whose very existence implies a separation from it. But it can be entered into in a deep mystical experience.

MM: *But there are certain concepts, aren't there, that can help us approach the mystery of the Mother?*

AH: Yes, if you see these concepts as fingers pointing to the cloudless full moon and not the moon itself. Very, very few mystics have ever known the Mother as profoundly and many-sidedly as Ramakrishna. He saw her as the shining energy of Brahman, the shining of the Source, the loving of Love, if you like, the Shakti, the force, that creates, sustains and destroys all things at all moments, flaming from and inseparable from Siva, the Father. For him, Mother and Father are inseparable. The Mother is to the Father as shining to diamond, he said, as the wriggling of a snake to the snake itself, as whiteness to milk. Ramakrishna didn't always refer to the Mother as *her*—this is very magical and important; sometimes he referred to the Mother as if she had no male or female side, or could be all sides at once. This refusal on his part to categorize in any human way the mystery of the Mother is revealing. As I said earlier when talking about the sacred feminine in general, the last thing that is needed now is a set of dogmas constellated around something defined as "the Mother" and, however subtly, excluding or denigrating "the Father" or the masculine. Paradoxically, adoring the Mother in this way would limit her and limit her healing power by substituting one sad narrowness and exaggeration for another. What Ramakrishna was witnessing, and passionately and tenderly calling the world to, was—is—a living experience of the Mother-aspect of God, of the peace, bliss, power and unity that is she, an experience immense enough to dissolve in awe and divine ecstasy all barriers and all categories whatsoever and to reveal the eternal, simple, burning sacredness of all things.

MM: *I accept what Ramakrishna is saying and see the need to keep all definitions of the Mother as open as possible. But aren't there characteristics of the Mother-force we can talk about? Isn't one helpful way of approaching the Mother to see her as the force in the Godhead which focuses and transmits just those powers of harmony, balance, peace and unconditional love that we were describing earlier as the sacred feminine?*

AH: Absolutely.

MM: *So the Mother-aspect of the Divine is what harmonizes and protects us and brings us into the peace of our real divine identity?*

AH: Yes, and also furnishes us the energy and wisdom to do divine transformational work on ourselves and in the world. The Divine Mother is the Godhead's face of love turned actively toward us.

MM: *And there is nothing whatever sentimental in this love.*

AH: The Mother is Kali as well as Mary. Her love can kill to create, destroy to rebuild or illumine. Death and suffering are part of her working.

MM: *Is there anger in the Mother?*

AH: Don't the earthquakes, climatic changes and natural disasters all over the globe show us that the earth our Mother is angry and getting angrier? But this anger of the Mother is a necessary stern warning, not a vengeance, an attempt to bring us to our senses and not a final judgment.

MM: *This brings me to what you said at the conclusion of our first conversation: that what Aurobindo taught you was that if there is to be a human future, it will wear the crown of female design. Exactly why is it so essential now to turn to the Divine Mother?*

AH: Because the Mother is unconditional endless love and the transforming force of endless unconditional love—the force, as Aurobindo realized, that could give us the confidence and power to go on, even in disaster. We need—all of us—the experience of that innermost blessing, love, more than anything else. We

have done incalculable harm to ourselves and to everything
around us largely because, as I have been saying, we have been
cut off for millennia from the holy experience of unity in the
Mother. In turning to the Divine Mother now, we open ourselves
again to the love that heals and saves. There is a great, ever-
increasing danger that as we wake up to the terror and desolation of what we have become and what we have done, shock will
deepen into terminal despair, apathy or even a kind of frenzy of
violence that could only speed up the destruction that is already
so far advanced. At such a moment, an image in the collective
psyche of a judging, angry, punitive Father-God is of less than
no help. Excessive guilt can only dishearten us. We need an
image of God that streams towards us—even now, even at this
late moment, even after all we have done— compassion, grace,
calm, humor, passionate and patient encouragement. This
image is the Divine Mother, and her force of love is the force
that, if we have real heartfelt contact with it, will give us the
force and the vision to go on.

MM: *Earlier when you were talking about the failure of the major religions, you*
      intimated that something of this image and vision is still to be found in them.

AH: In all of them, some glowing traces of the Mother have been
      preserved. Wherever there is a real mystical tradition, as I said,
      there is something of the presence of the sacred feminine,
      because the mystical adventure is rooted in continual receptiv-
      ity. But in each of the religions, this presence has been either
      repressed, half-denied or masked.

      Take the figure of Mary in Christianity. Mary has been given
      many titles and worshipped with sincerity, but she is never given
      parity with the Father. She is called the Mother of God but never
      the Divine Mother. In the last hundred and fifty years, the Virgin

has been appearing with astonishing regularity to people all over the world. The Church has been extremely slow to recognize these apparitions and officially acknowledge the increasing and passionate urgency of her messages to humankind. Then take the Trinity. It is often considered wholly masculine, which is absurd, although in the early Church, the Holy Ghost was worshipped as feminine, and certain fourteenth-century women mystics, such as Julian of Norwich and Mechthild of Magdeburg worshipped Christ as the Mother. Until the sacred feminine is invited into every aspect of the Trinity, until Mary is celebrated as the Divine Mother, until Christ is seen as a sacred androgyne—as much the child of the Divine Mother as of the Father, uniting the two in his being—until the mystics and the long and marvelously wise feminine tradition of alchemy are brought into the core of the Church's teaching, Christianity can never recover its sacred transforming force.

Let us look as well at Islam. Islam's greatest cultural periods were always when its mystical traditions, notably Sufism, flourished. The Sufis and other esoteric Islamic mystics have profound reverence for the sacred feminine, for the wives of the prophet who guarded his mystical oral tradition (the prophet himself said, "Paradise is at the feet of the mothers"), for the prophet's daughter Fatima, whose devotion to her father was revered and for Mary herself, archetype of highest surrender. In the poetry of Rumi and Attar, there is a vision of adoration of the Beloved that is feminine in the highest and most sacred sense. What is Rumi's work but a perpetual outpouring of the most abandoned ecstatic love, born from surrender? But this great vision of the feminine could not soften official Islam, with the tragic results we know. If Islam cannot renew itself by bathing in the living waters of its mystical tradition of the sacred feminine, it will continue to be a major destructive force.

In Judaism, although some of its mystical traditions have a vision of the Mother, of the feminine side or emanation of God—the Shekhinah—and also a vision of the holiness of everyday life once it has been sanctified by prayer, the religion itself remains strongly patriarchal, with an exaggerated emphasis on transcendence and law, and not particularly open to the insights and revelations of other religions.

MM: *But surely Buddhism and Hinduism have both preserved, to a large extent, a rich, many-sided vision of the sacred feminine? Think of Tara, the goddess of compassion, and the role she plays in Tibetan Buddhism and as Kwanyin in other forms of Mahayana. Think of the Hindu goddesses and how wonderfully, and with what subtlety and vitality, they represent different facets and different possibilities of the Mother, angry as well as tender ones, the full range of the feminine, with nothing softened or left out.*

AH: What you are saying is true. But in both Buddhism and Hinduism there remains, as I have said, a tendency to flee matter and this world and the processes of life itself, to see them as problems to be overcome, as illusions to be escaped from. And in this tendency there is a subtle and dangerous denial of an essential power of the sacred feminine, of the Mother as nature, as life, that we need desperately now. Neither Buddhism nor Hinduism have really developed the vision that Aurobindo gave to humankind—the Mother, the Shakti, as the force of evolution preparing a new world. Both of these ancient religions cling to a cyclical vision of time, which seems an unaffordable luxury now that time is visibly running out.

MM: *I remember your saying recently that of all the ancient major religions, it was in Taoism that you had come to feel most strongly the mystery and range of the sacred feminine.*

AH: If I had to give just two quotations from any religion that gave
     as far as possible a complete vision of the sacred feminine, it
     would be the following. They are both from Lao Tzu and express
     an amazing, inexhaustible subtlety and mystical intelligence. In
     the first, Lao Tzu says, "If the energy of heaven does not descend
     and the energy of earth does not ascend, then yin and yang do
     not commune, and myriad beings do not flourish." What better
     warning and inspiration could there be for the era of the sacred
     marriage? The second quotation from Lao Tzu gives, I think, a
     very full picture of the balance the Mother is trying to create in
     each of us and its marvelous result: "Know the male, but keep
     the female / So becoming a universal river-valley / Being the
     universal river-valley / One has the eternal virtue undimmed /
     And becomes again as a child." The sacred marriage of oppo-
     sites engenders in the depths of the being the sacred androgyne,
     the divine child, free from all definitions and all need for power,
     at one with the Tao, the Mother, in perfect, flowing, trust. It is a
     glorious and accurate vision, very close to that of the indigenous
     tribes of the world, to the aborigines, for example. It is, perhaps,
     the original wisdom of the Way. As well as Lao Tzu, I find the I
     Ching inexhaustibly useful and hear through its oracles the
     direct voice of the Mother. Its wisdom of humility, service,
     infinite attention and reverence to all manifestations of the
     Divine is saturated with the power of the sacred feminine. Used
     in the right way, the I Ching can be a guide from the Mother, a
     very sobering and illuminating guide, one whose ancient
     wisdom is eternally fresh.

MM: *But for you, I know, it is in Aurobindo that you have found the greatest and
     most expansive guide to what the Divine Mother is.*

AH: No one, not even Ramakrishna, has had a more glorious, open-
     ended vision of the Mother than Aurobindo. In him all the

visions of her from all the different traditions find their apo-
theosis, their consummation. I have never forgotten reading
these words one morning sixteen years ago in Pondicherry:
"There are three ways of being of the Mother of which you can
become aware when you enter into touch of oneness with the
conscious force that upholds us and the universe. Transcendent, the original supreme shakti, she stands above the worlds
and links the creation to the ever-unmanifest mystery of the
supreme. Universal, she creates all these beings and contains
and enters, supports and conducts all these million processes
and forces. Individual, she embodies the power of these vaster
ways of her existence, makes them living and near to us and
mediates between the human personality and the divine
nature."

For Aurobindo, the Divine Mother has four main cosmic personalities who have stood at the forefront in her guidance of this
universe and in her dealings with the terrestrial play; Maheswari,
Mahakali, Mahalakshmi and Mahasaraswati. Maheswari is her
personality of calm wideness, surpassing majesty and all-ruling
greatness. Mahakali embodies her power of splendid strength
and irresistible passion. Mahalakshmi is vivid and sweet and
wonderful with her deep secret of beauty. Mahasaraswati is
equipped with her close and profound capacity of intimate
knowledge and careful flawless work.

To this immense awareness of the many-sided glory of the
Mother, Aurobindo added one essential and revolutionary
ingredient: a vision of the Mother, the Shakti, as the force that
powers the evolution of the universe and as the force that would
sustain, encourage and create the next stage in the evolutionary
development of humankind. He realized the Mother as the
architect of evolution, the summoner of humanity to a supreme

and endless adventure of self-transformation. It is this extraordinary vision that Aurobindo explores in all its complexities and laws in his masterpiece *The Life Divine*, which is the greatest celebration of the Divine Mother and the sacred feminine ever imagined. What Aurobindo discovered was that by learning how to call down the light of the Mother and work with it in humility, flexibility and surrender, the entire spiritual and physical being of humanity could be transformed and the life divine lived on earth. Coming to know the Mother in this time, to know her power and how to work with it, is for him the clue to not only human survival but to the leap into divinity here on earth that is prepared already in the divine mind of God and which humankind now has to be brave and faithful enough to enact.

I believe that there are still endless discoveries to be made in and of the Mother. The human adventure into understanding the Mother is without end. Aurobindo would be the first to say that even *his* vision, all-inclusive though it seems, falls short of what she is, or can be realized to be. I have come to understand that knowing the Mother means being ready to transform anything you think you know about her at any moment; the knowledge of the Mother is as totally dynamic as she is, and as inexhaustible. Through her representatives on the earth at the moment the Divine Mother is showing the world that normal life is compatible with supreme realization and that direct mystical contact with the Divine can be sustained in any setting or activity. This is a revolution, for it dissolves all dogmas and hierarchies, all separations between ordinary and spiritual life, sacred and profane, humdrum and mystical. A new spiritual age has dawned for humankind, an age in which the Divine will be present intimately, normally, consciously in all things and activities and in which the divine life that Aurobindo wrote about so magnificently will be lived naturally on earth, as naturally as the

Mother's emissaries now live it, and with the same tenderness, tolerance, compassion, humor and reverence for every aspect of the creation.

MM: *Many mystics from all traditions—most notably, of course, Aurobindo— have claimed the Mother is bringing down a light, the light of the Absolute, whose presence now on earth makes the possibility of transformation on a world scale far more likely.*

AH: Frankly, Mark, if I had not, over many years and on innumerable different occasions, experienced myself the immense and extraordinary power of this light of the Mother, I would find it hard to believe in it. It is always hard to believe in miracles. Everything in the mind, in reason and unfortunately also in previous religious conditioning leads away from it, or tries to contain, mask, or flatten its impact. But the light *is* here, *is* working, and the miracle, too, is that anyone can open to it and experience it anywhere in the world once they have made a real contact with the Divine Mother in any of her forms. Thousands and thousands of people all over the world have felt this as-tounding power, and thousands more are certainly awakening to it as we speak.

The light is the light of the Absolute. It has always been here. The universe is burning in it. What the Mother is doing is, with total simplicity, making its power available, focusing it, and making it directly useful in all situations as a force of unprecedented transformatory power. The light has always been here, but never been used before. Like electricity, you could say, it is everywhere, but you must know how to *activate* it. This is what the Mother in all her forms is now doing. These are astonishing claims, but their truth has been experienced by many who encounter her with an open mind and heart. The Mother is nothing if not supremely practical. For an extreme disease, she has brought a power of extreme healing—the power of the ultimate light itself.

MM: *And this light could change history, alter evolution.*

AH: If we open to it. I can only witness what I know, through her grace. I believe, because I have, through the grace of the Mother, seen and felt the light many times, that the power of the light is beyond any human power to express, although I tried to describe my journey into it in her in *Hidden Journey*.

The great unprecedented spiritual leap that humankind will have to take fast to save itself and the planet could only be possible if there were a correspondingly vast concentration of divine power here on earth to make that leap possible and to give human beings everywhere every kind of inspiration, encouragement and help. That power, I believe, is the light now active, through the grace of the Mother, everywhere, all over the planet. Believe, know, the light is there. Call it to work in any path you take—Christian, Hindu, Taoist, Buddhist, any genuine path at all—and the Mother's light will take you with extraordinary intensity, efficiency and passion to the heart of the transformation you desire. I have seen this happen thousands of times in the lives of people of all kinds and spiritual persuasions.

Becoming aware of the miracle of the presence of this light, the revolution it is offering, its availability to anyone anywhere beyond all theologies and rituals and dogmas is, I have come to understand, essential for the survival and the transformation of the planet. The light has come up in an infinite dazzling sun, and its rays are penetrating everything, opening everything up.

But even this light of the absolute, focused for us here through the divine mind and the divine heart of the Mother, cannot and will not save us if we do not, as many of us as possible, turn with humility and sincerity to the Divine in whatever form we instinctually love most. The choice is still—and always is—ours. What more can the Mother of the universe do than come down in her various representatives directly to live with us, bringing with her the most direct possible forms of initiation and most powerful possible light and an unconditional passionate willingness to work with everyone, every religion and path on and in their own deepest terms? The infinite love of the Divine Mother is streaming towards us from all sides with unprecedented power. Learning to respond to it, in tenderness and trust, in courage and clarity of heart and mind and adoration could still, even at this late terrible moment, change everything and empower us directly to save the world.

Part Three

5

CHILDHOOD

Everything is prefigured even in the child; it must only be awakened and summoned forth in him.

—Paracelsus

MM: *You often call India your mother, the mother of your life. We've talked a little bit about your particular path as an Easterner educated in the West and attempting—in your own life—to bring about the synthesis described by Aurobindo. I've often thought of you as having a Western mind and an Eastern spirit. How did your childhood in India prefigure, do you think, the mystic journey you were to undertake?*

AH: It seems an exaggerated thing to say, but if I hadn't been born in India and spent the first nine years of my life there, I would probably be dead. My childhood in India has been the foundation of everything I have been and done, and its spiritual beauty has helped me survive the desolation and cynicism of the Western education I was given. In India, the idea that gods inhabit everything is natural. To the Indian, the world is magical and governed by magical powers, and from the beginning of my life, I was surrounded by people who accepted the world as a place suffused with mystery and divinity.

India is a place where many civilizations have crossed, where many worlds have risen and foundered. When I was a child, I felt this acutely, especially in Old Delhi, where there were Moghul and Turkish tombs. I remember being absorbed by the ruined beauty of those tombs; they gave me a sense that all human things pass away, that history is nothing but a record of the defeat of human ambitions and passions. "Everything passes away," says the Koran, "but the face of God."

I was born in 1952 and brought up by a part-Indian father and an English mother in the twilight of the Raj. The Raj ended in 1947, but the Indians still treated the English with exaggerated respect. Servants still dressed in turbans; the old English clubs still went on with their drinking and swimming pools and shining silver. There was something tragic and surreal about this atmosphere that has haunted me all my life. Since then I have never quite believed in any version of the world or society or progress that I have been given; I saw very young that everything human is transient theater.

MM: *As well as educating you in transience, India also gave you a sense of visionary beauty, of what Rilke called "sacramental perception"?*

AH: Being a child in India sharpens every sense. India is a tremendously sensual experience. A thousand memories rush back: The smell of eucalyptus drifting across the field in the place where I was at school. The taste of fresh mangoes brought up from the south to our breakfast table in Delhi. The smell of burnt earth after rain, of the open roof I danced on in the monsoon, of fish and egg curry when it's just heated, of my Ayah's sweat mingling with her lavender scent and the jasmine in her hair. This initiation into the erotic glory of the world is one of the things that made me a poet and a mystic. The reason I'm drawn to the Hindu version of God as Presence, as Mother, to the realization of everything as brimming and flowing with sacredness, is because of this sensual initiation as a child. In India, reality seems always about to break into flame.

MM: *India is sensual, as you say, but it is also horrific.*

AH: That's true. Being brought up in India as a child makes it impossible for one to view the world sentimentally. The horror of things is obvious. The poor sleeping under the bridges, the lepers in the streets, the smell of excrement, the hideous huts where people live such stricken lives, the omnipresence of death and disease, the horror of snakes writhing in the garden and stingrays hiding under sand. I remember lying in my mother's bed and hearing a howl fill the night. It was a rabid dog next door being tied to the back of a bicycle. I remember nothing except that its mouth was a mop of foam. For months afterwards I had dreams that the dog had been drowned in the river and those drinking from the river would also go mad. Soon after, in England, I saw a film about rabies, and I've never forgotten the naked, hysterical people leaping in mosquito nets in agony. From a very early age, my imagination was marked not only by the glory of everything, but also by the horror and by an obscure sense that the two were linked, were, in fact, one.

This understanding of horror has never left me. My imagination has always had an open wound in it. I'm grateful for that, because it's made the pain of things accessible to me. India's suffering is blatant, not hidden as it is in the West, swept away in hospitals and asylums. India's suffering walks the streets. You see the old mad women and the lepers with their great sores and the cripples wandering on one leg. You see the terrible strain of work on the faces of the rickshaw drivers and on their small muscles as they do this work that will kill them young. In one way that is terrifying, and in another way it's a relief, because the actual fact of life being suffering isn't hidden from you.

MM: *This initiation into pain balanced out the initiation into splendor, then?*

AH: More than that, India initiated me young into permanence. India taught me that there is something behind the different masks and theaters of pain, something behind both the splendor and the horror—something I could not articulate but felt as a mysterious presence. I remember sitting at four or five years old in an open room focusing sunlight on a piece of paper with a magnifying glass. At the moment the paper ignited, I went into a kind of trance; the silence of the room, the glittering of the glass, the fire and my state of concentration seemed to melt into one radiance. I remember many hours on a beach in South India, profound attention given to every crab, intense absorption in the sea wind, in the tawny shifting golds of the sands, being one with everything, beyond thoughts or words. This memory, vivid as a vision, is a clue and a sign on my search.

I first saw the Taj Mahal when I was six. I was taken by my father. I stood hardly able to move, gazing at it, in tears at its splendor. Nothing I had ever seen prepared me, or could have. The Moghul emperor Shah Jahan built it to mourn and celebrate his wife, Mumtaz Mahal, whom he loved, it is said in that wonderful phrase, "more than his own life." When she died, he was inconsolable and ransacked not only his own empire but the whole known world for the precious materials to build her memorial. The teak for the Taj's foundations came from forests in upper Burma, the pearls and rubies and diamonds and emeralds that adorned its facades from the Urals and Samarkand, China and Sri Lanka. Shah Jahan offered the beauty of the world to his dead wife, poured at her feet the skill, the virtuosity, the wealth of an entire culture. Gazing in wonder at that building as a child, I started to have an understanding, I think, of the wonder and extravagance of true devotion, and of the beauty that adoration of the feminine can give birth to. I believe my conscious journey into the Mother began at that moment, in that wonder.

6

REMINISCENCE

Remembrance makes people desire the journey: It makes them into travelers.

—Rumi

You have come from light and you will go back to light.

—Hindu yogi in
Pashupatinath
to Andrew Harvey

Each creature God made
Must live in its own nature;
How could I resist my nature
That lives for oneness with God?

—Mechthild of Magdeburg

MM: *At the core of devotion is the notion of reminiscence—the act of remembering one's origin. This return to Self is at the center of every mystic tradition and the primary aim of the spiritual journey.*

AH: When I was twenty-five and living at the Aurobindo ashram in Pondicherry, I had a dream vision that really shifted my life.

In this vision, I found myself in a cloud of light. Every atom was in the light and was singing this extraordinary clear music, all together. I cannot describe the power and the sweetness of that music. The words being sung were something like: I hate to leave you my Beloved, I hate to leave you. It was a burning sweetness coming out of the pain of saying farewell to God. I didn't realize why we were saying goodbye to God, but then I seemed to fall down a very dark chute, like a childhood slide. When I fell into matter, I awoke.

MM: *Coming into a body, we forget our divine nature.*

AH: This harsh and difficult descent into matter that the soul is making by taking on a body means that a certain oblivion takes place. Undoing that oblivion is the work of the journey. Plato talks about anamnesis, remembering of one's identity. What Socrates is doing to Plato is not teaching him something new, but through dialogue and the power of his presence, awakening in Plato a subtle memory of his origin. For Plato and all the Neoplatonic philosophers, especially Plotinus, and therefore for a whole rich school of Christian mysticism, what is actually happening here is that the soul, through different disciplines of prayer, is remembering its true nature, as veil after veil of ignorance and carnal stupidity is withdrawn through prayer and vision, until the soul rejoins the light which gave birth to it.

The Tibetans put it a slightly different way. A great master, Jamyang Khentse, said that through all the different lives that we live here, our essential Buddha Nature, a core of enlightenment, organizes all sorts of events, breaks and shatterings and revelations, so that we can recall that buried nature. Through life after life, opportunities, gaps, openings are given by this secret Buddha Nature to understand its place and to develop it. When we've become sufficiently conscious, through discipline and yearning, that Buddha Nature reveals itself in a master outside us. But what we meet in the master outside us is really our inner master. To enable us to remember that nature, we need the external image of the master which then awakens in stages, as in Platonic philosophy, an innate knowledge.

Again and again in the Hindu texts, you find the master saying that through discipline, through yoga, what you become is what you've always been. The task is not to do anything but to be what you really are.

MM: *Ramana Maharshi says, "What is on the day of laughter is also now."*

AH: The process of waking up in the dream of time to one's eternal identity brings a laugh of sudden remembrance. For me, the subtlest working out of this inner understanding of origin comes from the Sufi and Muslim philosophy. They have made it the very base of their mystic technology. What is called in Islam "the pact of Alast," or the primordial covenant, derives from something that God says to his creatures in pre-eternity. He says, "Am I not your lord?" and all the creatures say before they are actually created, "Yes, we acknowledge it."

Lahiji wrote, "The pact of Alast concerned all beings and was addressed to all beings and all recognized the sovereignty of God. However, since only man had the faculty of perfect awareness, and that it was to him that had been given the teaching of the names and the attributes, then it was him that was the real unfolder of consciousness."

As Rumi wrote: "We were made for your love, oh Lord, since pre-eternity. Since then we have been drunk, passionate, aware. Before the creation of the world and Adam, at the feast and the banquet of love, we were your companions and cups brimming with love." The Sufis know that what seems strangest to the eyes of the world, the Divine drunkenness of the mystic, is in fact the most essential part of our identity, one that has always been at the core of our being, beyond space and time since pre-eternity. This passion for Divine love is at the core of our identity. It is what makes us human; we are here to unravel and witness that passion. What happens in the relationship between master and disciple in Sufism is that this pre-eternal knowledge of passionate awakening is given back to the soul. The supreme dignity available to humanity is to be the companion of God at the banquet of love. This is the most dazzlingly optimistic vision of what human beings essentially are. It opens up to human beings a reascent into their true being, which is the fundamental movement of the cosmos.

The mystical traditions each in different ways tell us that we have come from light, and by devotion, adoration, purification, we are returning to light. God is flung out to the furthest reaches of the universe and is traveling back in human beings to God. God is doing this vast dance in the universe and in humanity.

Aurobindo, with his revolutionary vision of the Mother, brought new perception to this vision: that this return to origin will not simply be a return of the soul to the central point of unity. It will be a return of the whole of matter as well. All the other philosophies of reminiscence tend to leave out the earthly envelope, matter itself. In the Sufi, Hindu, Christian and Tibetan versions, it is the soul that returns to the Divine. The universe is seen as only a decoration for the soul, a school or threshing floor for its purification. Aurobindo's radical contribution was to imagine a return of the entire universe into its source—a divinization of the cosmos. The universe is by its nature divine, but matter is clearly very far from God in many ways. Aurobindo believed that Light would descend into matter from the Absolute to bring it up, through spirals of transformation, into divine unity. The aim of creation would be realized, he believed, by the whole universe blazing consciously in the light of God.

This is the most majestic vision that has ever been given to humankind of what the nature of the creation might be. A divinization of matter would be the foundation of a conscious divine life lived on earth, origin, source and reality becoming one. Aurobindo saw this merging as the unique work of the Mother, and realized that it is her love and its power that is drawing up the entire creation into its source.

MM: *Remembering Aurobindo's grand visions, let us return to how we are reminded in daily life of this origin and how it can help us along the path most of us are treading gradually, with very few visions and a very great need for more ordinary inspiration.*

AH: As Jamyang Khentse says, we are always being given hints about our origin. Unfortunately, in a culture like ours which represses transcendence, people are never given the authority to claim these hints and to acknowledge them for what they are. In a limited psychology such as ours, the most tawdry explanation of what these glimpses might be is given. Freud dismissed them as desires to regress to the womb. Jung never worked out what they were, although he talked very movingly about dreams and integration, about vision as the attempt of the psyche to heal itself. But what the mystics know is that these glimpses are very much deeper than that and must be worked with.

MM: *Many people have glimpses such as this, but they are not taught how to*

remember their sacred origin or how to work with the extraordinary insights
that are given them.

AH: People must awaken to the possibility of all of this going on in
their daily lives. This is happening all the time. As the Sufis have
pointed out, the world is being created and recreated in every
second. As Rumi says, at every moment, "a form has arisen out
of which has no form, and returned to there, for God has said, all
things come from him and return to him. So at each instant
there is for you a death and a return. Mohammed has said, the
world is only an instant. At each breath, we and the world renew
ourselves. However, we do not know this renewal and believe in
our permanence."

That description by a fourteenth-century mystic poet coincides
almost exactly with what modern physicists are telling us about
matter. At every second, there's an observable oscillation
between matter and nonmatter, life and death. If we are oscillating like this with the universe, at any moment the secret origin,
the secret nonbeing out of which all being is manifested, can
shine forth. Gerard Manley Hopkins says that "God's grandeur
will flame out like shining from shook foil." The entire universe
is shook foil. We're oscillating out of the primal ground of light
at every second. One of the rewards of the mystic life is to be
awake to this oscillation, to stop believing in the fiction of
permanence, to be aware of the universe trembling softly in the
embrace of nonbeing, the void which is manifesting everything.

We now need a philosophy that combines the most extravagant,
paradoxical discoveries of astrophysics and the ancient mystical
technologies to give modern humanity the most complete way
back and up; to give each human being the grandest possible
scale by which to understand his or her experience.

MM: *We're victims of a terrible theft, left with all of the suffering but with no transcendental context into which to put it. That's the source of Western nihilism. We're not instructed that suffering is a door to wisdom, that grace often works through loss, and that these are direct opportunities to grasp our true nature. There's a strange account of a woman telling the great saint Anandamayi Ma a terrible story about her life. Ma laughed and laughed until the tears flowed down her face. The woman was shocked and asked her why she was laughing at her misery. Anandamayi Ma said, "Because you are being shown the end of misery through the cracks that this misery is opening in your heart. Through them you can see the sun of the Self shining."*

AH: Exactly. You could say that samsara, this dimension of illusion, is designed to crack, to break. Loss, pain and death are cracks in the edifice of samsara through which we could see, if we were given the instruction, the light that is manifesting samsara. It is almost as if the rickety stage set splits to reveal the light that is behind it. The tragedy is that people have to face all the most serious things in their lives with no help. People face all the travail of bringing up children with no understanding of what children are, of where they come from. They face the pain of heartbreak, the horror of dying, without knowing that this devastation can be used to go deeper into the origin of all things. Human beings are deprived in our culture of all the tools which would help them endure, and transcend. Of course there's despair and a feeling of meaninglessness. Life is meaningless without the knowledge of our divine identity! Mystical vision and training give us the means through which to make that meaning active and vibrant. That is why mystics must be re-turned with full glory to the world. Without them humanity is a desolate orphan.

The Mother is here not only to bring back the understanding, but to awaken in humanity the faculty of search, the gnostic faculty that will remember the link between us and nature and God. The Mother is bringing back the memory of humanity. We have been through a huge accident—it's called nuclear—and our almost dead body is lying on a stretcher. Having almost been dismembered, our memory is also gone. As we lie on the stretcher we don't remember who we are, but the Mother is sitting by the bedside, and calmly, again and again, speaking our true sacred name. This healing is happening on a massive scale. A return to the memory of the race is what could save the world. When we remember who we are, we will see where we are. We will see that we are in the rose garden and that we are its guardians. We are in the place of the Divine theophany. We have been given the extraordinary dignity of being the interpreters, adorers and guardians of that place. When we remember, we will wake up to our transcendent responsibility to save the planet.

MM: *The Mother—the Master—holds up the mirror to remind us of our true nature. Sacred experiences and the contact with holy beings are the training ground for amnesiacs, a place to go to remember. In spiritual experience, there's always the sense of something intact being echoed. If I recognize anything of God, it's because I have that within myself.*

AH: Plotinus said that you cannot see the sun except with the eyes of the sun. Our task is to allow the light to bring the Self forward, to lead us back to who we are, to the home of our sacred origin. As the Shvetashvatara Upanishad says: "He who is in the sun, and in the fire, and in the heart of man is one. He who knows this is one with the one." And as the great gnostic text of the Oxyrhyncus manuscript puts it: "The kingdom of heaven is within you and whoever knows himself or herself will find it. And having found it, you will know yourselves that you are sons and daughters and heirs of the Almighty, and will know that you are in God and God is in you."

7

FEAR AND COURAGE

The ego is nothing but the coherence of the banal and of reactions against it…The ego has no part in any real world: our grave decorates an abstract landscape.

—Lewis Thompson,
"Mirror to the Light"

MM: *If the rewards of enlightenment are so sublime, why are human beings, as a rule, so ambivalent about it?*

AH: One day somebody came to the Buddha and asked him, "Why don't you give us liberation? You're always talking about it." The Buddha said, "Go around the city and ask at each house what everyone most wants, then come back and report what you find." Let's imagine what they found. Forty percent wanted a better job, forty percent wanted another romance, eighteen percent wanted peace of mind and the last two percent wanted to die because they were sick. Nobody wanted liberation.

One of the most upsetting things we unmask in ourselves as we become more conscious is a radical fear of freedom and joy. As Emily Dickinson wrote, "I can wade whole pools of grief but joy breaks my feet up." We learn to love our cage and to value the grim security our neuroses provide for us. Tagore wrote: "The shroud that covers me is a shroud of dust and death. I hate it yet hug it in love. My debts are large, my failures great, my shame secret and heavy, yet when I come to ask for my good, I quake in fear lest my prayer be granted."

MM: *One of the reasons that holiness is denigrated in our culture is that it sounds hokey, unrealistic. It's almost as if we're being lined up for execution, and somebody on line is dancing up and down, saying "We're not REALLY going to die, kids. God loves you!" As cynics, we have contempt for what seems bogus, as well as a fear of believing something we wish were true, but may not be. Most of us are so frightened inside that it's taken all the courage we have just to resign ourselves to the pain of life.*

AH: This resignation is killing the world.

MM: *Yes, but the last thing we want to hear is that all our depression might have been in vain. Besides, we're frightened of what enlightenment might cost and what we'd be forced to give up in the process.*

AH: A culture like ours which stresses desire and attachment so intensely makes cowards of us. Nisargadatta Maharaj puts it this way: "People just do not care to let go of everything. They do not know that the finite is the price of the infinite, as death is the price of immortality. Spiritual maturity lies in the readiness to let go of everything. The giving up is the first step, but the real giving up is in realizing that there is nothing to give up, for nothing is your own. It is like deep sleep. You do not give up your bed when you fall asleep. You just forget it."

Given the depth of the fear of freedom in the psyche, its subtlety and obstinacy, it seems to me that having and following a master can be essential. If we do so have we a chance of overcoming all the different ways in which this fear manifests. The master's love and spiritual power keeps us true to ourselves, despite ourselves.

There's a beautiful Sufi story I've always loved. A group of tigers in a forest leaves a tiger cub behind by mistake. The cub is brought up by sheep. The sheep teach it how to be a sheep. It walks like a sheep and baas like a sheep and eats grass. Many years later, a tiger happens to be passing and sees this ludicrous sight of a half-grown tiger behaving like a sheep. It is amused and saddened and drags the tiger to a pool in the forest. There, it shows the young tiger the reflection, and the tiger begins to wake up to what it really is. The older tiger teaches the younger tiger how to roar. At first, all it can do is make bleating sounds, but slowly the greater tiger-roar begins in its throat, and then after weeks of practice, it comes up to its master and gives the great roar of freedom.

Most of us are tigers pretending to be sheep—wild, totally free creatures pretending to be slaves of culture. But all of us can learn that roar of fearlessness. Tibetans call this the roar of the lion, which comes from understanding emptiness, knowing the void, seeing the interrelation of all things and realizing the inherent nonexistence of things. When you know emptiness, nothing can make you afraid.

MM: *Most people don't care about roaring, however. They're not seeking some final glory. They just want a little relief from the suffering of their lives.*

AH: That's true. The majority of spiritual aspirants I've met wanted not liberation but a manageable happiness. I'm certainly not condemning this, but unless we establish a firm understanding of the Self that stands beyond this pain, no temporary relief will provide the peace we're looking for.

MM: *There's also the fear of losing our individuality, the personal, soulful qualities that make us human.*

AH: It's helpful to make the distinction pointed to by all the mystical philosophies between what we might call "personhood" and the ego. Because we identify with the ego, the false self, we think that the false self is us. We're condemned to think that this selfish, haunted, hysterical being is all we are. What a condemnation, what a sadness, to confuse our true potential with this doomed being! That is the first and last illusion. As you wake up and the other, deeper mind emerges, you start to realize that the identification with this coagulation of habits which is the false self is, in fact, not true. There is a larger, more confident, more loving person there who uses your body and mind, who sees through your eyes, but who is as far from the false self as the false self is from a snail. When that person is discovered inside by the spiritual searcher, the identification with the ego is ended, with great relief. You step out of the prison into the sunlight.

MM: *And yet, in a mysterious way, one does remain oneself. Spiritual masters have very strong personalities, for example.*

AH: Rumi has a wonderful metaphor for what happens in the transformation. Say a dead horse is thrown into a lime pit. After some weeks, the bones and flesh of the horse dissolve, but its outline remains. That is what happens in the higher stages of mystical awakening; the outline of the ego is kept, but the power that is inside the ego comes from the Divine Self, which now uses the ego as a child would use a puppet. Ramakrishna said that he was a puppet in the hands of the Divine Mother.

The fear of losing the ego is its most resourceful way of remaining intact. It goes on playing baroque variations on that fear to keep you entrapped in its prison for as long as possible, but as the sense of bliss and freedom grows and deepens, the fear lessens and the relief is enormous.

It is very important to realize that there is a person inside who is not dying, who is not anxious, who doesn't need anything, who is calm, tender, confident and far more deeply himself or herself than this bundle of contradictions and repetitions we confuse with our truth. The one way to remember this person and your origin is through a sustained and patient practice of meditation. As you learn to slowly quiet the mind, your divine identity shyly steps forward.

I had a dream when I was twenty-five in Sri Lanka which I consider to be the truly initiatory dream of my life. I've found versions of it, almost verbatim, in Tibetan and Zoroastrian texts and was told it by an old yogi in the south of India, to whom it had happened also. In my dream I was sitting on a beach, and a very beautiful figure was coming towards me from far off. I couldn't tell if it was male or female, but it was radiant, had a golden face, and was gazing with great love at me. It came and sat down by me in the sand. We cradled each other in our arms, and then I found the courage to ask, Who are you? It smiled and said, I am you. At that moment, I woke up knowing that what I had met was my profound Self, my hidden Self, there behind all the different masks of Andrew Harvey. That initiation was the beginning of my search in India.

What we are here to do is to meet and become the person we are.

MM: *Let's get back to the fear of freedom. Are you saying that cowardice comes from an underlying suspicion, a dread deep within us, that we may not be who we think we are after all?*

AH: Yes. The cowardice comes from the fear I described of owning up to this essential unreality, this no-self. This fear echoes a deep truth that goes off in one life as madness or dementia and in another as enlightenment, given the right training. In one way, what a master can do is help us to go mad sanely, to break completely apart into the one, to see, know, and go into the void without any fear or panic, but great joy. This joy of course the ego has to resist, because it is its death.

MM: *I've become aware in my own journey of a saboteur that glimpses freedom then shrinks back and even pretends it isn't there. There's a fear that in facing the truth, we will lose everything—our position in the world, the connection with people we love.*

AH: This is every mystic's challenge. As soon as clear perception has any chance of taking hold, the saboteur is invited back in to destroy the spark. As soon as we're about to take flight, somebody reminds us that we will be the only bird in the sky. All the other birds will be on the ground dressing up in Armani jackets and swilling cocktails. Under the guise of truth, the saboteur depresses you so that you will stay on the ground.

MM: *That's where the leap of faith comes in. Before you have a communion with God, you have to be willing to leave the known for the unknown and risk being profoundly wrong.*

AH: Fear of renunciation is part of this cowardice.

MM: *But also, there's an innate fear of the light itself, that threatens to reveal everything. The light might challenge us to live and be the Divine Self.*

AH: Yes. We talk about wanting divine love, but in fact, a part of us is terrified of it, reels before the enormity of an unconditional eternal love. It takes many different kinds of courage to begin to admit it exists, and still more kinds of courage to open to it and finally embrace and become it.

A Jewish intellectual I know had gone to live in Hawaii with a local family. After several months, the head of the family told him that he wanted to introduce him to the family whale. He said there was a whale the family revered that would come when called to play with anyone in the clan, at a secret place on the island. They called the whale the mother of the family.

He thought they were crazy, but love gave him the courage to go to the secret place, a group of rocks in a bay. The trouble was, he couldn't swim. The father told him not to worry, to cling to a rock and let the whale do the rest. Before he could say no, they had him strip and lower his body into the water. The family started to sing.

Then, he said, the most astonishing thing happened. About five hundred yards away, the biggest black whale he'd ever seen calmly arose from the water. He was terrified, clinging to this tiny rock, and a part of him wanted to refuse the miracle and jump out of the water. But then he felt something that contradicted everything his rational mind told him was possible. He felt the whale feeling his terror and sending him great, warm, healing waves of pure energy. He says he knew with certainty that the whale could feel his fear, knew he couldn't swim and was sending him waves of what he could only call love, a strong, immense, impersonal love. Now his task was to stay in the water and receive that love—to trust and go on trusting.

The whale started to move, horizontally, very slowly and calmly, coming a few feet closer to him each time, so he wouldn't be swamped and drowned. He was overwhelmed and didn't know what to do. The head of the family said, "Go on, touch the Mother." Shaking a little, he put out his hand and touched her.

The whale rolled over onto her back and let him run his hand along her belly, as if he were her own child, nuzzling against her. Then, calmly, she withdrew.

He was no longer frightened. He had been healed of fear by wonder. He had *allowed* himself to be healed.

MM: *And so, with God?*

AH: And so with the Mother.

8

DEATH AND DEATHLESSNESS

MM: *It's common knowledge that all fears stem fundamentally from the fear of*
death. As Ernest Becker tells us, the ego is formed as a reaction to the child's
realization that he or she is in a dying body. Terrified, the child creates a false
self, a magical, immortal self, separated from all other selves in a self-
protected world.

AH: This is the root of our entanglement. The child looking in the
mirror for the first time realizes that this "thing" is what others
take to be itself. This cuts it off from its holistic understanding of
reality. The introduction of the mirror tells the child that it is
separate, and the child identifies with that separateness. These
two steps are part of the same alienation. Narcissism and the
denial of death arise together. They feed each other: narcissism
deepens as denial grows. As death creeps closer, narcissism has
to throw up more and more baroque fantasies to deal with
dying.

MM: *Life and death are both denied.*

AH: Yes. If you can't face death, you can't face life. And really facing
the horror and cruelty of death full on is very much harder than
almost anyone wants to admit. Yet if you can't face death, and
face it in its full terror and absence and mystery, fear of it dooms
you to a series of ever more desperate evasions. These evasions

come to constitute your identity, the false self with which you attempt, without any hope of success, to "manage" the mad precariousness of the world. This is one reason why it's best to start the spiritual journey young. In ancient cultures, people were initiated young into the harsh wisdom of death. Brahmans were taught from the time they were born about mortality. They were trained in the sacred texts before the evasions of the false self could develop. If you start the search at fifty, the evasions are more fixed and more difficult to overcome.

MM: *The avoidance of death through narcissism is also an avoidance of love.*

AH: Yes. The acceptance of love and the acceptance of death are part of the same movement. If we are all dying, how can we actually hate another person? If they are, as Sir Thomas More says, going in the same cart to execution? To see every other being as bound for death is to experience real compassion. And allowing that compassion to grow requires fearless openness to your own personal mortality.

When you awaken to the love of other beings, you awaken to the pain of dying. You awaken to the full sadness of time. That is why so many people will do almost anything to avoid love. What are promiscuous sex and the manipulation of other people but a way of avoiding the pain of love and death? Only facing the full pain of dying breaks the heart open.

MM: *Or armors it more securely.*

AH: In many cases, yes, since to face mortality is to face suffering and the full precariousness of loss, and to accept love is to accept the possibility of all those things. It seems easier to refuse the terms of reality. Narcissism is this refusal. Freud said that neurosis is the refusal to suffer. Narcissism is the master-piece of neurosis based on a steady strategy of refusal, rooted in unacknowledged fear which deepens as it's unexamined. Aging narcissists, which is what we're ruled by, are very dangerous people. As death approaches, their hunger for power and to prove their immortality gets more and more hysterical. They're willing to sacrifice more and more people on the altar of their own vanity. It's frightening to look at the majority of politicians and businessmen who rule the world because they are so clearly terrified. Their terror of losing power, and of death, makes them engines of destruction. Through this denial, they're even willing to institutionalize the death of the environment. This is the final paradox of narcissism, that it is willing to go on engineering total destruction in order to keep going and not have to face the shock and pain of truth; it will press the atomic button to keep alive its fiction of invincibility. It is as mad as that.

MM: *This madness is a natural consequence, isn't it, of the worship of a false self? Confronting death, the child imagines that there can't be a God, and so itself becomes God.*

AH: We make false idols of invulnerability and power which cannot possibly be real, existing, as we do, in a constantly precarious dimension. To sustain the reality of that fiction, we have to kill—emotionally, spiritually, physically, politically. It's like the monster in *Metropolis* which is fed bodies. You see it in sexual narcissists who need a fresh supply of victims.

What happens often at the beginning of the mystic journey is a shattering of narcissism—through nervous breakdowns, termi-nal illness, humiliations in love and so on—that forces us to begin to face the depths of our powerlessness in this dimension. Without wisdom, we are completely powerless; this is something everyone has to acknowledge. Without gnosis, we are helpless in the face of death. Only when the narcissistic dream is shattered can its whole elaborate fiction stand obvious in its poverty. This is achieved through disaster. Often, at the end of the incubation period of the search, the samsara of your life goes crazy. The film your illusions and fantasies and shadow are projecting gets madder and madder, until even you begin to see how your darkness is manifesting the disasters dancing around you. Until you begin really to fear the power of this inner darkness to go on creating for you pain after pain, you will not understand the relationship between your refusal of death and the continuation of suffering.

The Buddha's story is everyone's story. Here was a prince kept in an ideal world by a father who wished to avert the prophesy of his being a world religious leader, wishing him instead to be a conqueror. But when Buddha confronted the facts of time, sickness, death, the illusory world he was in was shattered. Then he saw a yogi who had attained serenity in the face of the frank acknowledgment of death, and that moment determined the Buddha's search. This story is archetypal. We try to live in an illusory world by various means, through art, sexual power, money—the cocktail is mixed in different ways—but if we're lucky, it will be a Molotov cocktail that blows up in our faces— the earlier in our lives the better—showing us that none of the evasions can be real, because we are dying. That fact makes all of our games pointless, futile, hollow and dreamlike.

The initial reaction to this may be fear and grief, but the same facts can be seen from a completely different perspective, as the source of an extraordinary liberty, an invitation into the perma-nence and glory of the self behind change. You come to ask: What is the force behind these shatterings? What is wearing

death like a mask? Only breakdown leads us to have to ask that
question and to begin to find the answer. The Buddha saw the
dead man and the eyes of the serene yogi at the same time. If we
look around us, we see the eyes of corpses and the eyes of the
Dalai Lama, of Ammachi at the same time. What do *they* know,
and how can we, too, know it?

MM: *The master incarnates the self-aware, enlightened self housed in a dying*
        body. Watching this paradox in action shows us a sane way of dealing with
        our mortality.

AH: The master is the Divine dying with us to show us how to live
        and how to die. One of Ramana Maharshi's disciples told me
        that when the Maharshi was dying, the disciple finally under-
        stood who he was; that his ultimate act of mercy, as an incarna-
        tion of Shiva, was to die with us. The last photographs of
        Anandamayi Ma are so piercing because they show us how
        extreme is the compassion of the Divine Mother. When she was
        utterly frail and worn away, she invited a few of her oldest
        disciples to sit by her bed, put them into a trance so that they
        lost consciousness and when they awoke, she'd left her body.
        She enacted the complete *lila* and turned the final act of desola-
        tion, as Christ did, into a sign of her and everyone's ultimate
        mastery.

MM: *On her deathbed, Anandamayi Ma told her disciples that nothing in fact*
        was changing. "What is happening is the pull of the Unmanifest (Avyakta),"
        she said. "All that you notice is due to that."

AH: The summer before my Tibetan master Thuksey Rinpoche died—
        he was already extremely weak—the radiance and joy streaming
        from him were shattering to any understanding of life or death
        I'd had before. During one of the long life ceremonies in his

honor, Thuksey Rinpoche had to kneel down before Drukchen Rinpoche. Nobody thought that he was strong enough to do it. Everybody was terrified, but he managed it, although in obvious pain. He bent his head and as he got up, the entire room rang with this immense sound which everyone heard. The Tibetan word for emptiness, *tongpanyid*, shook the walls of the room. I hadn't even imagined that such things could happen, but they do. We all heard it.

Later, I was walking in the hills. The figure of Thuksey Rinpoche that had been used in the ceremony was lying on a rock. It had lost its head; the robe had come undone. As I watched the headless figure baking in the sun, I heard again the word *tongpanyid*. I realized that the person I had thought of as "Thuksey Rinpoche" had already "died" and gone into absolute reality. I was identifying with a past form, and he was giving me this hilarious teaching. That night, on the mountain outside Hemis, I heard all the rocks singing around the monastery; I was told that this was a traditional sign of enlightenment. Since that time, I have known literally that the deathless state exists.

Many years later, I met the monk who had been with Rinpoche when he was dying. We sat in Leh in a room filled with sunlight, talking quietly about his death. Thuksey Rinpoche died smiling between two breaths. He held his breath, went into meditation and left his body. Then "he" returned. Three years later, "he" was reborn in an area outside Ladakh. His incarnation has been recognized and is now living with Drukchen Rinpoche in Darjeeling.

It was because I realized that the Tibetans really know how to die that I collaborated with Sogyal Rinpoche on *The Tibetan Book of Living and Dying*. I wanted the West to have access to the extraordinary Tibetan knowledge of dying. In some ways, more than any other mystic technology, the Tibetans can help us to understand death.

MM: *Why is Buddhism in general so useful in understanding death?*

AH: Buddhism's sobriety and scientific purity begins with an unsparing awareness of impermanence. This is the first and last Buddhist teaching. Before leaving the body, the Buddha said, "All compounded things decay. Work out your salvation with diligence." For the Buddhist, the continual and ruthless focus on impermanence is what gives urgency, passion and clarity to the spiritual search, and what slowly initiates the mind into the deathless state. That is why the search for eternal life can only go through the door of death. As one great Tibetan master was dying, he motioned a sobbing disciple to come to him in his death throes and whispered, "Nothing happens." He was resting in the state of deathlessness and letting the body fall away.

When Ramana Maharshi's disciples begged him not to leave them, he said, "Where would I go?" The deathless ones, the bodhisattvas, are here in ways that none of us are yet. Rumi is here in a way that the old woman on the street is not. It's so strange to realize that the real world is full of morose ghosts, identified with precisely those things in themselves which are unreal, while reality is full of the presences of the things we don't normally see. That invisible world is what the mystic wakes up to. A Sufi master says that nonbeing, which is what we're in, reflects the sun of the Absolute. You can't look at the sun directly; you have to look at its reflection in a puddle. But the mystic learns to grow the kind of eyes that can look directly at the sun.

MM: *Is this what is meant by mystic death?*

AH: Of course. You can only see the sun directly if the false self has
died. And to die out in life for the love of God, as Mother Teresa
is doing, is the most beautiful life there is. It is to be the source
of endless joy and inspiration. Mother Teresa says that we can
live in heaven now, but we must live as Christ lived. "We all long
for heaven where God is," she says, "but we have it in our power
to be in heaven with Him at this very moment. But being happy
with Him now means: loving as He loves; helping as He helps;
giving as He gives; serving as He serves; rescuing as He rescues;
being with Him twenty-four hours; touching him in his distress-
ing disguise."

This slavery to Love is the source of all real power and of
deathlessness. Mechthild of Magdeburg wrote on her tomb-
stone, *Bei Nichts Stan—Zu Niemand Gan* (Standing by Nothing, I
go to No One). To accept annihilation in the light and to work is
the slave's joy, for what the light kills, it rebirths. In mystical
transformation, you are feeding your being to the light, and
every part it eats, it makes immortal. Mystical life is radiant
cannibalism, offering yourself up again and again as food for the
light. The light won't eat you unless you've been made tasty
through prayer, through adoration. Adoration spices the being
so the light can eat you; it prepares the meat of the ego. It is the
wine the Self drinks as it eats the old self. Your adoration makes
God drunk enough to eat you and make you eternal.

MM: *So you are saying that one reason the mystic has to begin by accepting*
death is that he or she will have to die so many times.

AH: Before you become deathless, you need to have been purified
completely. Rumi says that to make a great sword, it has to be

plunged seven times into boiling water. The Damascene silver requires that kind of savage tempering. He said that the divine being is like leather, which has to be left out in the desert sun a long time to get that toughness and pliability, that rugged yet supple quality it needs to endure. After accepting the fact of physical mortality, the other, more serious deaths begin.

MM: *You're saying that physical death and the death of the false self are compara-*
bly catastrophic?

AH: Deathlessness is hidden at the center of the house. You have to be killed in every room of the house before you can get to the room where deathlessness is. That is the glory of the process. The mercy is that after the first couple of killings, you know that you're being killed into life. You begin to participate in the killing willingly. People go into retreat to die in another room, to come closer to that center of deathlessness. Everyone doing a serious yoga with a master or with God directly is learning how to die in life, how to die *into* life. They know that the law is that the more you die, the more you live.

MM: *How is it possible to grasp fully the prospect of enlightenment without*
acknowledging also the laws of karma and reincarnation?

AH: It's very difficult, because it is hard to imagine that a state so vast and complete, which involves the destruction of so many barriers and the opening of so many centers, could be achieved in one lifetime. It can be, we are told, but it's very difficult. Reincarnation makes so much sense on so many levels that it's time that it was accepted.

MM: *What are the consequences of the fact that most Westerners do not accept*
these laws?

AH: I think the two principal barriers to enlightened action in the West are the inability to comprehend the law of karma and the inability to accept the law of reincarnation. If the West really understood karma—that every action has a corresponding reaction, and that anything done to another or to nature will have its direct consequences sooner or later—then a true sense of responsibility would be born in every Western heart and mind. If we accepted reincarnation, then the desperation that most Westerners feel, that this is the only life, everything has to be had now, grab it while you can—the whole nihilistic and hedonistic philosophy—would be undercut at its very root. This hectic pleasure-seeking, which breeds a tragic despair and irresponsibility toward other people and the planet, would be dissolved.

If we understood the relationship between karma and reincarnation (that we are reincarnated to work off negative karma, to purify ourselves and to enter increasingly into enlightenment), a wholly different attitude would come about. Reincarnation was accepted by Christianity until the sixth century. There is evidence of this in the gnostic gospels, early Church fathers like Origen and many of the Christian sects. Christ, who may have been taught in the Mahayana universities of India, might himself have believed in reincarnation. Many of the parables of the Buddha find extraordinary parallels in Christ's parables. I think belief in reincarnation was scrapped by the Christians because it interfered with the power of empire and Church. The Church's hierarchy is much more powerful if there is only one life and they are the only mediators of grace.

MM: *What might the right relationship with the body be like, for example, with this understanding of reincarnation?*

AH: One way of looking at the body is to see that it is given to us to
        be taken away, and so to compel us toward liberation. We have
        a bomb ticking within us which is called death. After a while you
        hear the ticking of that bomb as it grows louder as you grow
        older. The ticking is there to remind you to transcend your iden-
        tification with the body, to go beyond the body while you're in it.
        Otherwise, the body will explode in your face in the darkness,
        and you will know nothing. That is the amazing relation we have
        with this time-bomb body which will explode at any moment
        and blow us into a dimension of which we have no knowledge.
        Unless we know what death is while we are in the body, we're
        going to go into a darkness we don't understand. What the
        mystic does is to remain alive while dead and dead while alive,
        to burn steadily in the fire beyond what we call "life" and what
        we call "death."

        Living in this fire and as this fire, the realized mystic experiences
        time as a Divine Being. God is at once transcendent and imma-
        nent, eternal and dying and burning away in time. The enlight-
        ened being is taken into a supreme simultaneous ecstatic
        experience of all possible modes of being. The Gita says: "When
        one sees eternity in things that pass away and infinity in finite
        things, then one has pure knowledge." The Mundaka Upanishad
        explains: "And when That is seen in its immanence and tran-
        scendence, then the ties that have bound the heart are unloos-
        ened, the doubts of the mind vanish and the law of karma works
        no more." The Isa Upanishad puts it with an even more adaman-
        tine clarity: "He or she who knows both the transcendent and
        the immanent, with the immanent overcomes death and with
        the transcendent reaches immortality."

MM: *This is what the Hindus call* sahaja, *and the Buddhists* nirvana, *and the*
        Sufis baqa, *"remaining in God."*

AH: Yes.

MM: *But for those still on the spiritual path and not at the end of it, nothing is more essential than meditations on death.*

AH: You must think every day that you might not make it to the night, so that everything you do could have the beauty and serenity that you would bring to an action if you were dying. A tremendous gentleness is born from daily meditation on this.

MM: *And gratitude. "If the cardinal's flight from bank to bank were less brief, it would also be less glorious," said a medieval monk.*

AH: If you really know that you are dying and really know that every second you are closer to death, then everything that happens in time becomes delicate, refined, transparent; every sight and smell and encounter becomes sacred, taking place in a dimension that is visibly arising and disappearing. Everything reveals itself as so fragile that your heart opens. That is what the enlightened heart is: total openness without fear to the poignant evanescence of everything. Rumi wrote: "The soul's extravagance is endless: spring after spring after spring...we are your gardens dying, blossoming." And: "To die in life is to become life. The wind stops skirting you and enters. All the roses, suddenly, are blooming in your skull."

9

LAZINESS AND DISCIPLINE

MM: *To reach this state, however, the emphasis must be on practice, not on supernatural experience. Each of us must meet the Self through some form of practice or meditation. And yet, at the pace most of us live, an inner mystic discipline can be difficult to maintain. We're addicted to fast solutions, and yet so much of spiritual life happens mysteriously, with a rhythm of its own and not according to the dictates of our will.*

AH: I like what Nisargadatta Maharaj, one of the greatest Advaita masters of this century, says on this subject. In one of the dialogues, a Westerner talking to him about mantra asks, "How can dull repetition and boredom verging on despair be effective?"

Maharaj answers, "The very facts of repetition, of struggling on and on, and of endurance and perseverance, in spite of boredom, despair and complete lack of conviction, are really crucial. They are not important by themselves, but the sincerity behind them is all-important. There must be a push from within and a pull from without."

He adds, "What prevents you from knowing is not the lack of opportunity, but the lack of ability to focus in your mind what you want to understand. If you could but keep in mind what you do not know, it would reveal to you its secrets. But if you are shallow and impatient, not earnest enough to look and wait, you are like a child crying for the moon."

This makes me think of nearly all the Westerners I know, including myself. Sogyal Rinpoche calls this phenomenon "active laziness." We're trained to divert ourselves from seriousness. Our society is built on distraction which, as we've said, is an expression of the nihilism and despair that underlies a culture which thinks that because there is nothing to be gained or understood, all that we can do for a dying animal is to offer it a few pleasures between the meaninglessness of birth and death.

This condemnation to distraction is very difficult to overcome. Anyone undertaking the seriousness of the spiritual quest will have to fight strongly against it. Active laziness gives us every excuse not to sit down to pray, not to meditate, not to give to our relationships the kind of work that they need.

So much of what is essential in the spiritual life is to relax, to let go, to rest in the nature of mind. Then you are no longer straining. Westerners have this damaging belief that spirituality is as strained, hectic and self-torturing an activity as jogging or crawling up the corporate ladder. We use the same kind of fevered will, and lack fundamental trust in the love and wisdom of the Divine. This is, in fact, another facet of active laziness, because the most transformative discipline may be not to "work" for a while, so as to allow yourself to rest in the silence of the love of God, and to allow the eternal wisdom of that silence to guide you forward. Whenever I remember what the great Sufi master Bistami said, I return to peace and to a balance between striving and trust, effort and profound rest. "At the beginning [of my spiritual search]," Bistami wrote, "I concerned myself to remember God, to know Him, to love Him and to seek Him.

When I had come to the end, I saw that He had remembered me before I had remembered Him, that His knowledge of me had preceded my knowledge of Him, that His love towards me had existed before my love to Him and He had sought me before I sought Him." Knowing what Bistami came to know, knowing that through meditation and contemplation, is what infuses practice with a deeper and deeper natural happiness and spontaneous gratitude.

MM: *Let us return to laziness for a moment. It seems to me that so-called laziness is tied very deeply to self-loathing. We're taught from childhood that we are essentially lazy, and that in order to work, we must whip ourselves into action.*

AH: And that simply being is shameful. Our society is obsessed with "action" and tells us that we do not exist if we do not act; that we have no right to be unless we do.

MM: *Discipline is a double-edged sword. We need it for spiritual progress, yet our negative associations can taint our understanding of what discipline—which comes from the Latin root "to learn"—actually is. Many of us have been encouraged to use discipline as a punishment, as a torture, rather than viewing it as a friend. Laziness continues partly because we're trained to be in opposition to ourselves. It's a reaction against the inner tyrant, the child saying no.*

AH: Yet in some ways this society works very hard. People in corporations put in eighteen-hour days without blinking. But they spend little time on the only serious activity there is: namely, finding out and experiencing the nature of reality. Ramakrishna said that if only people put as much time into searching for God as they spend hunting for sex and money, they'd be enlightened in no time.

MM: *Yes. But this effort can easily turn into spiritual materialism and ambition, can't it? We turn enlightenment into another commodity, another pursuit. We parade our spiritual lives the way we parade our Porsches, and we forget that the goal of spiritual life is peace.*

AH: Ramana Maharshi said that the awakened person is like a child drowsily drinking milk from the breast of the mother—a state of supreme contentment, silence and relaxation. Dzogchen talks about the self-delighted state of being free, of flowing like water from moment to moment.

To reach that final state, an enormous amount of work has to be undertaken. What is needed is a paradoxical mixture of intense effort and effortlessness, of discipline and abandon. Each seeker has to understand this paradox, in terms of his or her own temperament. You must learn how to play yourself, just as a sitarist knows exactly how to play his or her instrument. There are times when you need to focus, to fast, to retreat, and others when you need to play. The seeker has to know, like a doctor, what remedy is most effective for every nuance of illness. This requires suppleness and the outwitting of whatever fantasy you are threatened with at the moment. If you are in a bout of self-righteousness and want to do five thousand prostrations, it might be better to get drunk. In that frame of mind, you will only reinforce spiritual pride. If your chief desire is to be distracted, better to stay in the room and say your mantra until that frivolous desire subsides. You need to recognize at each moment what brings you back into the central state. Every seeker needs an array of different techniques—not just one. Rumi said that a true spiritual seeker is a pharmacist of bliss. Imagine that in the pharmacy there are five hundred different vials, one is marked "Aretha Franklin," another marked "meditation," another "talking long-distance with one's best friend," another is "reading Nisargadatta Maharaj in the bath." At any moment, the practiced seeker will know exactly which vial to mix with which. You become the inner inventor of your own joy. The whole of your life becomes a way of helping yourself by innumerable means to enter your deep Self.

MM: *What role does the master play in all this? Is he or she the chief pharmacist?*

AH: I asked a realized master once how you can tell if you're in the presence of an enlightened being. She looked at me and said, "By the bliss." That direct connection gives mystical encourage-ment, tastes of divine love. Ramana Maharshi talks about feeling, in the presence of the master, the fragrant winds of the Self blow over you. The master can give you enough bliss to help you to strive and to go on showing you in his or her being what joy awaits you at the end of all your striving.

People who undertake something as complex and demanding as the spiritual process alone are noble but can be misguided. Part of the delusion of the West's cult of individualism is the mis-taken belief that everyone already knows what God is and how to get to God, that this knowledge is immediately accessible, that they can do it simply on their own. It's like trying to become a surgeon from reading medical books or learning Japanese from just looking at the characters. Picasso said that at twelve he could draw like Raphael, but that he had spent all his life trying to draw like a child. In all the arts, simplicity and spontaneity are the rewards of decades of discipline. Why should this not also apply to the supreme art, enlightened living?

MM: *One of the greatest paradoxes on the journey is knowing how much help we need just to become who we are. What is your main discipline?*

AH: Essentially, my discipline is to let all thoughts dissolve as they arise in their source, the self. That is sometimes difficult beyond belief. There are moments when I would rather be working in a coal mine.

MM: *I use the question, "Who Am I?" the* advaita vichara, *to center myself. Many masters suggest* japa, *repeating a favorite name of God, as the simplest, most direct, most effective method, one that can be done anywhere, by anyone, at any time—the clue to the transformation in fact.*

AH: Absolutely. Its results are astonishing. Ramakrishna said that "Japa means silently repeating God's name in solitude. When you chant his name with single-minded devotion, you can see God's form and realize him. Suppose there is a piece of timber sunk in the water of the Ganges and fastened with a chain to the bank. You proceed link to link, holding to the chain, and you dive into the water and follow the chain. Finally, you are able to reach the timber. In the same way, by repeating God's name, you become absorbed in him and finally realize him."

All the major mystical traditions, Christian, Sufi, Hindu and Buddhist, use their own versions of the repetition of the name of God as the most effective path to entering the presence of the Divine. To say the mantra or prayer from the depths of your heart, at any moment, wherever you are, recollecting yourself with great love and devotion, keeping in mind the master or aspect of God you're devoted to, gives you immediate access to the power. Each divine name is full of divine vibrations that surround and penetrate both our bodies and our whole inner being. Until I began to try it seriously, I had no conception of how extremely effective it was. There is vast inner power in *japa*, and the marvel is you can do it anywhere—on the bus, by the sink, on the phone. *Japa* can thread all moments together and reveal their unity, because the sacred name you choose is always there, repeating. The whole of life becomes a raga of adoration. The Divine Presence you have invoked so simply surrounds and sustains you and fills you with its energy of rich joy.

MM: *I have found that the best way to practice is to dedicate its benefits to the welfare of other beings.*

AH: Yes, because that dissolves your attachment to enlightenment and arouses what in Buddhism is called *bodhicitta*, the great compassion for all suffering human beings around you. I shall never forget Thuksey Rinpoche speaking to me for the first time in Shey monastery about *bodhicitta*. The light was falling on his face and the room was filled with exultation. "Without great compassion," he said, "no real progress on the spiritual path can be made." Arousing that infinite love in the heart will give you the energy to practice; you will understand its universal purpose. You radiate your prayers to the beings of all four directions. The more you give away, the wider your heart becomes and the more divine joy can be poured into it. Eventually there is just a receiving and a giving; that's all an enlightened being is, a transparent diamond wire through which the electricity of divine consciousness and love is passing without effort all the time. To reach this state requires constant consecration of every gift to the joy of all other beings. Out of this consecration, I find, an atmosphere of the most vivid imaginable inspiration is created.

MM: *Which many rigorous disciplines sorely lack.*

AH: So many people don't know *how* to inspire themselves. Use everything that moves you: music, walking by water, flowers, photographs of the enlightened ones. Inspiration helps so deeply in overcoming laziness, summons what the Sufis call the fragrance of the Beloved into everything.

MM: *Mother was once asked by an atheist what to do if you don't believe in God. She replied that everyone loves something. To find the sources of your love is crucial to remaining inspired.*

AH: Each person has been given a key to his or her own door which opens directly on to enlightenment. An old woman once came to Ramakrishna and said, "I can't do any spiritual discipline and can't pray—I'm completely hopeless." He smiled, took her hand and asked her who she loved the most. The woman's face lit up and she told him about her little granddaughter. Ramakrishna told her to meditate on her granddaughter, love her as divine and her life would be filled with light.

MM: *There seems to be a danger of becoming a dilettante if you see yourself as a pharmacist of bliss, however.*

AH: Yes, there is a danger of what Sogyal Rinpoche calls a "shopping mentality." Given the shortness of human life and the infinite variety of possibilities, it's most important to choose one that corresponds to your deepest temperament and possibility and really follow it. All the masters agree that the essential thing is to master one way, one path, with all your heart right to the end, while remaining open and respecting the insights of all others. The Tibetans say, "By really knowing one path, we accomplish all."

There's a laziness that arises out of the multiplicity of options. When you have a world that combines tremendous distraction with an overwhelming variety of options, you have a very dangerous situation in which people can easily get lost. My advice for someone beginning is to meet as many masters as possible and come to a sense of what path suits your temperament best and who can guide you most deeply or go to God directly.

MM: *Meher Baba said, "Dig in one place."*

AH: Yes. The modern fantasy that we can always keep all our options open and never need dedicate ourselves to anything is one of the stupidest illusions of our culture and one of the ego's most ingenious ways of sabotaging our spiritual progress. Commitment in love and spiritual life are nearly identical. How can you know about love until you've chosen one person to try to love, in time, with all the difficulties, and accepted that love can only take place in the atmosphere of fidelity and commitment? Accepting the limitations is what allows you to transcend them. Any teacher, for example, will necessarily have certain limitations to the observing eye. Dwelling on them can be very destructive. It's important to be faithful to your teacher above and beyond everything because when you're tempted to be "unfaithful," you're most likely being distracted by illusion.

MM: *That doesn't mean overlooking obvious abuses.*

AH: The Tibetans talk about testing a teacher for twelve years before becoming a disciple. Nothing could be more important. But having made your choice, stick with it. You will go on being tempted to stray. But often you're projecting faults or weaknesses or difficulties or vanities which are often due more to you than to your teacher. With a teacher whose powers have been proved, and whom you trust, the connection should be honored as far as possible. It is your channel to illumination.

MM: *And with the honoring of that connection, practice becomes easier and constantly more fulfilling and illuminating.*

AH: A subtle wonderful balance develops in the seeker between detachment and intense dedication. Practice becomes a move-

ment of serene passion. At this stage the whole being of the
seeker begins to burn. I love this story from the Desert Fathers:
Abbot Lot came to Father Joseph and said, "Father, according as
I am able, I keep my little rule, and my little fast, my prayer,
meditation and contemplative silence. And according as I am
able I strive to cleanse my heart of thoughts. Now what more
should I do?" The elder rose up in reply and stretched out his
hands to heaven, and his fingers became like ten lamps of fire.
He said, "Why not be totally changed into fire?"

10

OCCULT AND MIRACLES

MM: *We have been talking about the genuine wonders of mystic life. Let's say a*
        little now about the "false" ones. There seems to be an inordinate interest
        these days in the supernatural—miracles, occult practices, paranormal
        phenomena and so on, which have little to do with the rigorous transforma-
        tion called for in genuine spiritual practice.

AH: That cannot be said enough. Ramakrishna tells a marvelous
        story about two disciples of a great master. They made a pact
        that they would meet in ten years' time and tell each other of
        their spiritual progress. When they did, one disciple said that
        he'd become a little bit more patient. The other man smirked
        and said, "Instead of taking the ferry, I just walk across the river."
        "How much does that cost?" asked the first man. "One anna," he
        answered. "You mean to say that you've spent ten years saving
        yourself two annas a day?"

        This story underscores the limitation of occult powers. The aim
        of mystical transformation is to end the round of birth and
        death, to stop the wheel, to enter into permanent possession of
        your Divine Selfhood and to ascend out of the nightmare of
        samsara. Occult power can keep you trapped in the illusion of
        your power instead of releasing you.

MM: *In fact, true mysticism and the use of magic or occult powers are antithetical.*

One is about receiving, the other about offering.

AH: Yes, the mystic unites the will with the emotions in a passionate hunger to go beyond the world of the senses so that the Self can be united by love to an object worthy of love. However, in magic and the pursuit of occult powers, the will unites with the intellect out of a hunger for knowledge and the power it can bring.

MM: *This is intellectual, aggressive and an extension of the scientific temperament trying to take one into another dimension.*

AH: In some mystical disciplines, occult power is said to be the most dangerous of all possible temptations. Any mystic who is going through a process will be given very strong occult powers from time to time. He or she will become aware of clairvoyance, telepathic influence. I myself have been tempted in this way at certain moments of my journey with my master. Every time, I heard her say, "Give these up, they will block you. If you play with them at all, you will be burnt to death by them." I gave them up at every stage that they appeared to me. That is true of every serious mystic. We realize that what the ego will do is appropriate these powers to keep itself alive. It will smuggle itself in as the emperor of the occult and use that to establish another empire even more dangerous than its original one.

As Evelyn Underhill so beautifully says, "Mysticism is essentially a movement of the heart seeking…to surrender to ultimate Reality; for no personal gain; to satisfy no transcendental curiosity, to obtain no otherworldly favour….but purely from an instinct of love." In this lies the great difference between mysticism and occult powers. The mystic is passionately in love with the Absolute not in any sentimental way but in what deserves to be called a heroic way because he or she accepts all the ordeals on the road to union. The practice of occult powers does not entail this kind of devotion or rigor. The magician is after his or her own purposes, playing God like Prospero in *The Tempest*. Whatever good the magician may want to do is thus inherently tainted, can never have the free, astonishing sweep of grace.

MM: *It's essential to remember this in materialistic times like ours. Many people feel desperately impotent and are, therefore, fascinated by all sorts of technology. Witness the prevalence of Satanic cults, for example.*

AH: What people want from Satanic cults is what they want from society in general. They sacrifice a child to get a new house. They burn the hands off a newborn baby to get a new car. They subject their children to molestation and terrible abuse, ritually and together, so that they will rise in the corporate hierarchy. What these horrors demonstrate is the length to which the degradation of this culture's values have gone.

MM: *Fundamentally, cultists are doing in appalling actuality what many people are doing psychically anyway.*

AH: People express great horror at these cults, but why don't they express horror at the culture that these cults are mirroring and paying black tribute to? The way of the mystic transformation is the exact reverse of the way of power. It is the way of surrender, of love. The paradox, as we've said, is that the power that can then play through us far surpasses anything that the ego or the will can engender. Without taking very seriously the warnings of the great saints like Ramakrishna, the energy of the transformation could be derailed to another form of materialism.

MM: *The materialism of these cults is profoundly linked to evil.*

AH: Yes, but it must be fought with love, not with hatred, as the Dhammapada reminds us. By hating evil, you contribute to the absence of light, not the other way around. Hatred of evil does not diminish evil; it increases it. When you hate, you bring the suffering of hatred upon yourself. If you strike without compassion against the darkness, you yourself enter the darkness. These false ways and visions can best be countered by living unwaveringly in the light. This brings me to miracles.

MM: *Can the obsession with miracles be misconstrued as yet another form of "divine" materialism?*

AH: I have seen what could be called miracles, of healing, of transformation, happen around several masters. They never, in my experience, claim them. The great healer Shantih, who initiated me as a child in India, never claimed it was her power; it was always Krishna who was curing. She'd had an experience of dying in another life, of going to Krishna, who told her to return to the earth to tell people what she'd learned and that he would give her healing powers so that people would know that his presence was in her. Any real healer knows that he or she is being used as an instrument.

Around the awakened Self, miracles dance naturally. Healings take place and revelations occur quite simply, like the heat in a pot cooks vegetables.

MM: *The word* miracle *may itself be misleading.*

AH: There's the limitation of language again. If we are basically divine and if our identity is essentially beyond space and time, if what the mystics tell us is true and by this process we can attain unity with the Divine, then many of the unconditioned powers of

God at moments of grace flow through us. Those powers are in the nature of God, which has its own laws. What we call *miracles* are the workings of those divine laws in reality.

The Buddha defrocked a monk for doing a miracle, saying that he was not in the business of miracles and that any yogi after a certain stage can do them. What he was after was the real miracle, a change of heart. The birth of real knowledge is the real miracle. A Tibetan monk, Terton Sogyal, once said that floating on the ceiling and walking through walls is all very well, but the real miracle is the change of one negative habit. Of course, it may be important for certain avatars like Christ to do miracles to show that the Divine is present and can alter the laws of so-called reality at will, but our fascination with those miracles can be negative if it stops at the miracles themselves and doesn't go deeper into what those miracles imply.

MM: *So often when Christ has done a miracle, he tells his followers to go and repent for their sins and change their lives. The miracle is not the end; the transformation that takes place afterwards is the essential point.*

AH: For me, the last darshan of the Buddha shows us the true miracle. When the Buddha was dying, he brought his monks together. Everyone went into contemplation, waiting for him to speak, to give his final message. Instead of speaking, he held up a flower. One monk, Kasyapa, smiled and attained enlighten-ment. To Kasyapa he gave the charge of the teachings.

What did the Buddha mean? Surely that the cosmos was itself the miracle; the flower is the miracle; the fact that we can sit in this room and talk about these things is the miracle. Those roses expanding in water in front of us are the miracle. The miracle is the freshness and astonishment of each passing moment, the perfume of what the Sufis call the ageless rose of reality.

MM: *The mind of the prophet is the theater of the mysteries of the presence of the love of God. Rumi said, "In that theater, everything is appearing as miracle, always."*

AH: The realized mystic is what the French call *eperdu*, drunk, lost in splendor. There's a Sufi saint who used to go into ecstasy seeing one rose. His disciples would try to clear all the flowers out of the room, otherwise they wouldn't get any teaching! If his eyes strayed to one of the ragged flowers in the bowls in the corner, he would be out for the rest of the afternoon. He was truly present at the miraculous feast of the Mother, and knew the truth of what Rumi wrote at the end of his life: "The law of wonder rules my life at last. In each leaping second I live afresh."

11

VISIONS

Eternity was manifest in the light of the day, and something infinite behind everything appeared: which tallied with my expectation and moved my desire.

—Traherne

Be careful, O friend! Fall in love not with love, or its visions, but with the Beloved.

—Rumi

MM: *William James wrote that the "conscious person is continuous with the wider self through which saving experiences come." Visions are examples of such saving experiences and serve a crucial purpose in mystical awakening.*

AH: True, but allowing visionary ecstasy to swamp active love is a mystical vice. Visions are a means but not the end; the end is the kind of passionate, energetic life we see in the lives of the great mystics such as Teresa of Avila. No one could have had more visions than she did. She was, however, a very practical woman. When the visions happened to her, she opened to them completely, absorbed them, meditated on them. But she didn't sit about having her soul pierced by the divine fire. She walked the length and breadth of Spain founding nunneries and fighting the Church.

I love Teresa for her exasperation with her own visionary faculties. There's a story about her telling the nuns that if she began
to levitate during Mass, they should grab hold of her so she
wouldn't fly off.

After having her vision of Christ in a train, another Teresa,
Mother Teresa of Calcutta, didn't stay in that state; she used it
to fire fifty years of charity working with the poor of Calcutta.
Visions are given as inspiration to work both on ourselves and
for the Beloved. We remember St. Francis not just as the person
who received the stigmata and talked to the birds, but as the
person who founded the Franciscan order and lived a life
exemplary for its sanity, passion and purity. His visionary life
gave him extreme stamina. Visions, when they are authentic,
give an uncanny strength in daily life. The Sufis say that the
highest state of all is an external sobriety coupled with an inner
overwhelmedness.

MM: *You talk about seeing the light. Is this a literal experience for you?*

AH: Yes. When the mind opens in the mystical awakening, and when
the eye of the heart opens after sufficient gnostic instruction,
you see the divine light with open eyes. This slowly becomes a
normal experience. The Mundaka Upanishad says that "This
invisible Atman can be seen by the mind, wherein the five
senses are resting. All mind is woven with the senses, but in a
pure mind shines the light of the Self." When the Tibetans
describe the "Ground Luminosity," they are talking about a
literal experience of this light. When the mind becomes subtle
and peaceful and transparent enough, it sees the divine light
radiant in everything, as the ground and essence of all things.
What mystics of all traditions know, feel and see in their purified
hearts and minds has rarely been better or more exactly de-

scribed than by the Christian mystic Ruysbroeck: "When love has carried us above all things. . .we receive in peace the incomprehensible light, enfolding us and penetrating us. What is this light, if it be not a contemplation of the Infinite, and an intuition of eternity? We see that which we are, and we are that which we see: because our being, without losing anything of its own personality, becomes one with the Divine Truth." Ruysbroeck adds: "[The contemplative] finds himself and feels himself to be that light gazing *at* that light, *by* that light, and *in* that light. Here one has entered totally into the godhead and one knows in the light and by the light."

This is an accurate description by a supreme scientist of the soul. Coming to see this light gives complete certainty. When that light reveals itself as present in all things normally, how can you doubt that you are the Self and that everyone and everything else is too?

MM: *Have you always seen this light and now understand its source, or is it a new experience?*

AH: It's a new experience. The senses change in the mystic journey. Sight, for example, becomes much more acute and much more gentle. Do you know the painting of St. Francis by Bellini in which every detail has an almost hallucinatory precision? That is how the mystic comes to see reality. A totally different vision slowly grows, a much greater clarity and purity that has within and inseparable from it the intense sweetness of love. The old barriers between "within" and "without" dissolve and what is within you surrounds you in calm glory.

This state sounds very grand but is in fact the normal state of the individual, and everyone's secretly in it without suspecting.

Everyone can see this if they only allow the peace of their essential natures to be revealed and recognize and find the world shining in it. When the light is first unveiled in the mind, it is amazing. Then you begin to practice living in the light quite normally and understand why the masters stress that you have always had it. You realize that all your life you have been like a woman running frantically around the house looking for the diamond necklace that is around her neck.

MM: *In a way, you don't become illumined. You just stop imagining you're in the dark. You mentioned the senses just now. Could you say more about how this illumination affects perception?*

AH: One of the "Hadiths" of Mohammed has God say of the true believer, "I become his eye by which he sees, his ear by which he hears, his hands by which he holds." What this means is that the ordinary senses become saturated, irradiated and luminous with the divine presence. The self that is always using the senses anyway unveils its working in each of them and so what was ordinary sensory experience becomes subtly and constantly ecstatic.

There's a story of Rumi walking with one of the disciples; hearing a door scrape and a windmill turn, he went into ecstasy because all they were saying was, "Allah, Allah." You begin to penetrate into that mind where all sounds are mantra, all sounds the love cries of silence.

Touch, too, becomes consciously holy. I understand a little now why it's said in Buddhist texts that in heaven people make love simply by touching fingertips. Their refinement is so extreme, their purity so passionate, that touch is all they need to attain union.

MM: *Let's get back to the light. Would you describe it as precisely as possible?*

AH: The divine light is colorless, a calm light like that of the dawn,
        which does not hurt the eyes. It is sober and has no emotional
        coloration. There are other kinds of divine light of all shades of
        the spectrum, and they can come accompanied by ecstasy. They
        all arise out of the white light and have different properties,
        functions and powers. In fact, the whole universe is constantly
        being created out of the play of these different lights. These
        lights with their powers have been described in all the major
        mystical traditions, Sufi, Hindu, Mahayana Buddhist. For me the
        clearest description of them and their working comes from a
        thirteenth century Sufi, Najm Al-Din Kubra, who writes: "There
        are lights that ascend and lights that descend. The ascending
        lights are the lights of the heart; the descending lights are those
        of the throne (the Godhead). The false self is the veil between
        the throne and the heart. When this veil is rent and a door
        opens in the heart, like springs toward like. Light rises towards
        light and light comes down upon light." "And it is light upon
        light (Koran 24:35)." It is time that the West accepted descrip-
        tions such as this one as scientific in their dimension, as
        scientific, in fact, as Einstein's theory of relativity. The corre-
        spondences between the different traditions' descriptions of
        these lights are too uncanny to be coincidence.

MM: *Do you literally see the different lights with open eyes?*

AH: Yes, some of them. These experiences are completely natural,
        but when described to an age like this, they seem hallucinatory.
        In fact, when they happen, they are always normal although
        astounding. One day, perhaps, people will see divine light as
        they eat their breakfast and that will be the beginning of sanity
        in the world.

MM: *And yet, you claim never to have had the predisposition to this understanding.*

AH: I never thought that I would have any visionary experience. I didn't have any psychic gifts or any sense that I was a mystic. Although I was an artist and a poet dwelling deeply in my imagination, visionary potential depends on the grace of God or the master. God or the master opens the visionary eyes, although some people are more available to such openings than others.

I think that I was given so many visions because I was so stubborn, hard-headed and vain. My master hit me gently over the head again and again to make it impossible for me to deny truth. She knew that I would run away from the grandeur of what truth is. Every time I fled, she gave me a vision of greater intensity. It was her game with me, and it showed me that it was divine grace, not my "talent," that created these experiences. I want people to know that these visions came to someone unwilling to receive them. They menaced my version of reality for a long time.

A real vision happens in a realm beyond anything that the imagination can produce. A vision has much greater intensity than a dream, for example, and seems to take place in complete lucidity. The hallmarks of vision are inescapability and clarity. One of the mystic's tasks is to stop the imagination from conscripting the vision or coloring it in any way. Fidelity to the vision is crucial and frightening; otherwise you are in danger of losing its reality.

MM: *We began this conversation with your talking about the danger of too great an emphasis on visionary experience. Anandamayi Ma points out that "if after coming down from contemplation you have not been transformed, the contemplation has not been real."*

AH: Yes, because if the vision is authentic, what you have tasted is something of the glory and greatness of God. A real vision brings adoration of the Divine, and in that adoration there can be no vanity. Visions are helpful, and you must be grateful for them. They are signs, they deepen faith, they show you what you must aim for. But the real work is building love, true clarity and silence, in illumining the whole ground of your character and mind.

I have had many visions since *Hidden Journey*, but the difference now is that I do not take them with the same degree of seriousness. What matters is the daily ordinary progression in virtue, tenderness, and direct action. I learned that addiction to vision can end in a subtle grief, in which you are longing for bliss, like the laboratory rat longs for the injection of cocaine, and miss life. For quite a long time, I saw spiritual practice as a way of entering visionary ecstasy. Later I came to understand that the visions were to make me a better friend and citizen and to give me the courage for action in the world.

MM: *Let's get back to opening initially to the visionary experience. It took me a long time to begin to throw away doubt and the fear of losing control, in order to entertain the possibility that these things are possible. What data can we use to guide us sanely in this dimension?*

AH: Look at the great mystic technologies. Read the Tibetan texts, the Upanishads, the Sufi masters, read Eckhart and St. John of the Cross. They give very distinct guidelines. The Upanishads, for example, list the various sounds heard in meditation. When such experiences start happening to you, and they will, you won't think that they're illusions. You'll have the appropriate scientific attitude toward them. The Divine is deeply mysterious, but it has laws with which you come to cooperate.

Many of the initial signs are subtle. The way in which God comes into a life in the beginning stages of opening are gentle. God approaches the human self with infinite delicacy. If you're not attuned or trying to be receptive, you may miss so many of these openings.

MM: *One frustrating thing for people who aren't having visionary experience is that you cannot contest its veracity.*

AH: But there is, as I've said, a whole very precise and sober vision-ary literature of which people are ignorant. If you read Mircea Eliade's essay on mystical light, for example, you see that he's bringing together many different traditions in which the light clearly appears, from monks in Alexandria to shamans in Siberia. The existence of the light, as I've said, is one of the facts of humanity. Instead of calling it incontestable and subjective, let's put it into the realm where it belongs, the objective. We have to accept visionary experiences as an objective fact of the mind and find out what they are revealing. What is the mystical faculty of perception? Is it just a phosphorescent disease of the mind? Or is it actually a door opening onto the transcendent? Make up your mind, because what you decide will decide the whole of your life. Are near-death experiences, as some fright-ened scientists are claiming, just the last secretion of the chemicals in our blood that pacify us as we go into oblivion, or are they actual encounters with a different dimension? I've met at least twenty people who've had such experiences whose lives have really been changed.

Again, if visionary powers were confined to a few, there would be something suspicious about them. In fact, they're not. They are our birthright, as natural as breathing. Under the guidance of a real master, or with the sudden grace of God, anyone can develop them. But then, as an old Indian yogi once said, "Once you have seen God, you have to become one with God." And that costs everything, because it is beyond price.

12

HUMILITY

A young man asked an old rabbi: "In the past, in the wonderful old days, we have heard that people used to see God with their own eyes. God used to walk on earth and call people by their name. God was very close. What has happened now? Why can't I see God? Why has he forgotten the earth? Why does he not hold the hands of people stumbling in the dark?"

The old rabbi looked at the disciple and said, "My son, God is still where he used to be, but man has forgotten how to stoop down low enough to see him."

—Hasidic story

Humility is the queen without whom none can checkmate the divine king.

—Teresa of Avila

MM: The highest price in spiritual life is paid, of course, in the ego's currency. For this, radical humility is necessary.

AH: The masters of all the mystical traditions have taught that there can be no divine knowledge and no mystical awakening without radical humility. Each human being goes through a door to the kingdom of God. This door is exactly as high as you are when you walk on your knees. If, in the pride of the ego, you stand up straight, you cannot fit.

MM: *God simply will not appear except to those who are lost in love for God.*

AH: Yes. The mystery of the divine presence is ringed about by fire, like Brunnhilde in the myth of the Nibelungen. Only the humble are ever allowed to go through and embrace truth in its living form. In this way, there is no possibility at any time of the highest truth being abused, exploited or domineered by the arrogant.

MM: *The really great saints and yogis are always the most humble. Unless you are humble, the Divine will not use you.*

AH: Humility is the prerequisite for the experience of God. The real reason for this is that the Divine itself is finally humble, far more so than human beings, because it is dying in everything that is and existing always in a state of perfect and all-embracing love. This is extremely hard for the intellect or the ego to understand, for these faculties can only imagine power in terms of domination and never in terms of the tenderest and most exposed selflessness; this law of humility then is not something imposed on the creation. It radiates in undying splendor from the essence of the divine being itself.

Angela da Foligno expresses this marvelously in an account of one of her visions:

> The eyes of my soul were opened, and I beheld the
> plenitude of God, wherein I did comprehend the
> whole world, both here and beyond the sea, and
> the abyss and ocean and all things. In all these
> things I beheld naught save the divine power, in a
> manner assuredly indescribable; so that through
> excess of marveling the soul cried with a loud voice,
> saying "this whole world is full of God!" Wherefore I

now comprehended how small a thing is the whole
world, that is to say both here and beyond the
seas…and that the power of god exceeds and fills
all. Then He said unto me: "I have shown thee
something of my power…." He then said, "Behold
now my humility." Then I was given an insight into
the deep humility of God towards man. And
comprehending that unspeakable power and
beholding that deep humility, my soul marveled
greatly, and did esteem itself to be nothing at all.

The gap between what Angela da Foligno is telling us and the
intelligence of our culture is frightening. A civilization like ours
can only be demonic, because it is ignoring the fundamental
principles of interdependence and mutual honor that underlie
and sustain the creation. In the I Ching, the luckiest hexagram is
considered to be Number 15, Modesty. This is not simply
because modesty is the most attractive of the virtues; it is
because it is the essence of God and nature: "It is the law of
heaven to make fullness empty and to make full what is modest.
It is the law of earth to alter the full and to contribute to the
modest. High mountains are worn down by the waters, and the
valleys are filled up…when a man holds a high position but is
nevertheless modest, he shines with the light of wisdom."
Humility, then, is the natural response to the laws of nature and
so the shining of wisdom herself.

MM: *People of all paths know that the hallmark of holiness is humility. It is*
obvious in all the greatest masters.

AH: The I Ching also says, "If a person would rule, he or she must
first learn to serve." Spiritual royalty can only be attained by
those who've stripped themselves of all pretension. The crown

of union will only be placed on the head of a mystic when he or
she has been stripped of everything but love of the Divine.
Teresa of Avila only attained the mystic union at the end of her
life, because by that time, she was worn away, clear, humble
enough to be given the ultimate identity. Ultimate power can only
be given to those who do not really exist. How could enlightenment be handed over by the power that is the universe except to
the one who is most obedient, gentle, loving, empty? Only that
person could not under any circumstance abuse those powers.
Only humility can create the absence in which the Presence can
install itself. Only humility can create that peace in the heart that
is the mother of flexibility and divine skill. As a Taoist master
Chen Ting-Van wrote, "The mind of the sage is empty and calm,
profoundly calm, dealing with the world harmoniously, like
bellows taking in air, like pipes containing music."

MM: *Humility is the most terrifying of virtues for many Westerners because it
takes away all the ego's props and reveals all its games without exception.
This stripping runs counter to what we're taught in this system about
control, competition and the nature of success.*

AH: Yet it is pride that keeps us slaves in the camp. This is the
saddest paradox, and since all forms of pride can only be
destroyed by life—pride in body, pride in possessions, pride in
mind—a system rooted in pride is rooted in the weakest, most
self-destructive force of all.

Every genuine mystical experience does two things simultaneously; it initiates you into your deep identity and eats away
another fantasy of your false one. This is why a culture like ours
is terrified of the mystical; it reverses everything we've been
taught and reveals the truth of the definition by Ramana
Maharshi of education as "learned ignorance." The ego wants to

say, I am—run and control everything. The mystic longs only to say, I have passed away; only you live in me. In this state, humility is no longer an issue.

MM: *An old Indian master once said, "Humility is knowing exactly who you are."*

AH: Yes. Once you have seen, in Buddhist terms, that the Void is manifesting everything and that everything is interconnected; or in Sufi terms, that all things that exist are atoms dancing in the fire of the Beloved; or in Christian terms, that all things are Christ, and that He is the secret link and identity of all things; or in Hindu terms, that all things are Brahman, then any clinging to the personality and its goals and prejudices and passions becomes ridiculous. You know beyond doubt that anything you are is entirely a focusing of divine energy through you. You become aware of your complete dependence on the divine energy for everything you are. Everything is flowing from the Divine and you derive your entire being from God. Realization brings the paradox of being completely majestic and completely humble, of being the entire cosmos and nothing.

MM: *Just as God is both everything and nothing, dying and immortal, in time and eternity, all at once and simultaneously.*

AH: Exactly.

MM: *Because we live in a secular society, we have an alienated, rigid, cartoonish image of what holiness and its attributes, such as humility, should look like. The self-mortifying Christian hangover has left us with a bitter taste in our mouths, believing that only self-loathing is humble. We never think of humility as festive or majestic.*

AH: Humility is a source of true joy, and it is tragic that people

interpret it so often in a debased "Christian" sense. People have
had humility rammed down their throats as piety or self-
mortification. That is a barren vision. Why not talk about it as
the opening of a window onto rapture, as a condition of the
clearest and deepest knowing? Any progress in humility is
automatically a progress in joy.

For one thing, humility is the source of gratitude, itself an unfail-
ing spring of delight. As Thomas Traherne said, "There is a disease
in him who despiseth present mercies, which till it be cured, he
can never be happy." Humility is sensitivity to "present mercies," is
being "present" to the mercies of the present, the love that the
light is streaming towards us at all times in all conditions.

Yet, it is sometimes hard to see from the outside who is humble
and who is not, for real humility obeys none of the laws that the
ego would like to impose upon it. We imagine a false humility,
that a humble person is cringing and crushed, but that is simply
the projection of the ego. A truly humble person can seem to the
ego ferocious, crazy or arrogant, when in reality he or she may
be speaking from the ground of enlightenment and acting
passionately on behalf of the Divine in all beings. This can be
the mystic predicament. The Sufi saint Al-Hallaj was drawn and
quartered for proclaiming, "I am the Supreme Reality."

MM: *This was interpreted as megalomaniac blasphemy.*

AH: Yes, but as Rumi points out in the *Table Talk*, this was not Al-
       Hallaj speaking, but God in and through him. Of course, this
       kind of what you might call "divine pride" is only possible in the
       highest state of union.

MM: *Imitations of it can be dangerous, particularly in times like these where there*

are so many false prophets. Surely, it's better to err on the side of caution
and visible humility.

AH: Of course. That is why most masters strongly recommend that
        right up till the state of union with the Absolute, we should
        preserve a sense of duality, being the servant or the child of
        God. Ramakrishna prayed to the Divine Mother again and again,
        "Oh, Mother, take thy virtue, take thy vice, and give me pure love
        for thee. Here, take thy knowledge, take thy ignorance and give
        me pure love for thee." The only position that is free from the
        danger of either self-loathing or inflation is the humble position
        of motiveless, stainless love for God. Through the transparence
        that this radical humility brings, far more can be accomplished
        by the Divine through you.

MM: *This is another paradox, that humility is the source of a strength, energy,*
        stamina and insight that the ego cannot possibly imagine, since it's free of
        selfishness.

AH: The root of humility is the Latin *humus*, which is "earth." To be
        humble is to be grounded, and to be grounded is to be strong.

MM: *How then would you define a divine pride that is not harmful?*

AH: I would say that real divine pride is a natural emanation of true
        humility. It is refusing to act in the world as anything less than
        your real self, refusing calmly to accept the definitions a secular
        society or tyrants or power-hungry gurus of any kind impose on
        you, witnessing, despite everything, your identity as a divine
        child of the Divine Mother. This witnessing is never personal; it
        is on behalf of everyone. Because that recognition can be very
        threatening to the status quo, many individuals who've stood up
        for divine pride throughout history have been hated or mocked.

As T. S. Eliot wrote, "In a world of fugitives, those taking the opposite direction will always be said to be running away."

MM: *Let us return to what you were saying about humility being the prerequisite of mystic understanding. In the process of unlearning falsehood, we have to be able to admit—and go on admitting—how little we know, to cultivate the openness of a beginner's mind.*

AH: The truth is that learning and humility in the dimension of reality are the same process. Wisdom is knowing at each moment that you do not know so the Mother can lead you forward into true knowledge, stage by stage. If you're not prepared to give up at every moment what you've learned, you will be satisfied with minor realizations, not free to go on and on into an endless expansion of awareness.

Another essential aspect of humility on the mystical path is to keep you attentive to the signs that reality and its constantly shifting synchronicities are always sending you. To the rational mind, this kind of attentiveness to things that it disregards completely looks like psychosis, but to one waking up to the interdependence of all things, to the always interlinked signs and events in the universe, it is not only common sense but an indispensable form of protection of the truth that is being born in you. This form of humility is the midwife of exactly those kinds of moral and spiritual vigilance that prevent the false self from appropriating vision and knowledge for its own ends. The ego imagines that enlightened power offers us unlimited license; the contrary is true. Enlightened awareness shows itself in an intensely scrupulous obedience to all the particulars of reality. The ego is in a dream of omnipotence. The enlightened spirit, on the other hand, is always listening to what reality is saying. As the Tibetan master Padmasambhava says, "Though my view is as spacious as the sky, my actions and respect for cause and effect are as fine as grains of flour." Why do the Tibetans do divinations before making decisions? Because they are humble enough to be alert to the fact that the universe is shifting at all moments.

MM: *Shifting and interrelated. Scientists are now discovering in quantum physics and ecology how completely everything is interrelated. One of the challenges of the next stage of evolution is for Westerners to take the ethics and responsibility of scientific discovery far more seriously and put them into practice.*

AH: The Western models of understanding are faulty because they leave out two essential things: the awareness of the heart—its power to awaken and illumine the mind—and the awareness central to all sacred traditions—that the person who knows the most knows that he or she knows nothing and so can be constantly open to being taught. Although nearly all the great figures of Western science, such as Newton, Einstein and Heisenberg, have been humble, the technological society built on their discoveries has been fantastically arrogant. Tuning perception constantly by mystery and wonder, realizing that what we don't know may always remain unknowable, letting the universe slowly reveal itself to us, respecting the web of interbeing that it and we are, are essential now for our survival.

MM: *Nearly all mystical traditions have stressed commitment to a master. Devotion to the master can be the most direct and powerful way of safeguarding this essential kind of humility. Until enlightenment, it's crucial that we remain accountable to a higher—and wiser—authority.*

AH: I know that whatever happens there will always be an abyss between my master and myself. I find this hopeful and inspiring, not discouraging in any way, for it shows me that enlightenment

is an endless process and gives me the confidence to know that
wherever I am, she will always be light-years ahead, gesturing
me forward in a smile of light. This is the sweetness of the great
game, and humility is what enables us to play it and go on
playing it forever in always expanding dimensions.

At the end of his life, Dilgo Khentse Rinpoche, acknowledged as
a living Buddha by the whole of the Tibetan world, signed his
last letter to Sogyal Rinpoche, "My master Jamyang Rinpoche's
worst disciple." Just as every true artist knows that he or she will
never realize completely their vision, every spiritual seeker
knows that there's a perfection beyond the perfection that he or
she has grasped.

MM: *And yet, perfectionism can so easily be twisted into a form of cruelty.*

AH: This is false perfectionism and stems from lack of understanding. Real understanding makes us humble enough to see the
grandeur of the attempts of other people, to bless and encourage them when they fail. Only when you learn humility do you
appreciate just how hard other people are trying. Only when you
start really to learn humility do you start to practice what the
masters are always practicing, seeing people in their perfection,
praising them for the letters of the alphabet of awareness that
they've got right. Everyone, after all, is fighting so much inner
darkness, grief, ignorance, pain. False perfectionism causes a
profound depression, since you and nobody else can live up to
these imaginary standards. It keeps you in a spin of self-hatred
and condemnation of others and is the source of both subtle
and blatant violence. To see the world through the eyes of
humility, however, changes everything.

MM: *Even evil?*

AH: Yes. Humility and love offer a release to all those in that cramp
       of self-hatred that is the source of so much evil. This is part of
       the secret relationship between humility and evil, that where
       piety cannot get through to it, somebody who comes and sits
       humbly amongst the criminal can break their hearts. The only
       way to break the heart of evil is to love humbly and uncondi-
       tionally, as Christ did. Even the most hardened and vicious
       torturer could feel the simple, childlike goodness of the Dalai
       Lama. Anyone, regardless of his crimes, could come into
       Ammachi's presence, feel her unconditional acceptance and
       know that he or she was not being judged. Humility before the
       sacredness of the other always holds out the possibility to
       change, for it knows that the wounded need more love than
       anyone. "For in truth," says the Dhammapada, "in this world,
       hatred is not appeased by hatred. Hatred is appeased by love
       alone. This is the eternal law."

13

GRIEF AND THE NEW THERAPY

The king's son lives in the dark depths of the seas, as though dead, but yet lives and calls from the deep: "Whosoever will free me from the waters and carry me to dry land, him will I prosper with everlasting riches."

—Alchemical Text

Pain will be born from that look cast inside yourself and this pain will make you go behind the veil.

—Rumi

MM: *The therapist Ariel Jordan says that there is no healing, spiritual or otherwise, without grieving. He compares it to a cup that has to be emptied before new experience can be added. Many spiritual seekers are carrying a lifetime of unexamined grief inside themselves. How would you say that acknowledgment of grief corresponds to the path of expanding consciousness?*

AH: A culture that bans transcendence also bans grief. A culture that represses mystical love represses that grief that can be the source of opening toward that love. We're carrying around lifetimes of grief, and one of the hardest things to do in a culture like ours is to admit to the depth of the pain inside us.

From all sides we're told lies: about our identity, about the solutions to our problems, about the glory of success. Those lies are institutionalized by the media and divorce us from our grief, widening the abyss between our conscious minds and the ache that is fueling our drives. This is why it often requires some kind of breakdown for this appalling facade of lies to be cracked open. When they glimpse the pain they are carrying around, many people are so terrified that they rush back to the lie, bouncing from one false solution to another. The pain has to be so great as to make that evasion impossible for there to be a real chance of healing.

Rumi says, "Desperation, let me always know how to welcome you, and put in your hands the torch to burn down the house."

MM: *The role of grief in spiritual traditions is ambiguous, however. Certain of the cheaper versions of religion, for example, suggest bypassing grief altogether and marching straight into the light. Then, pain will end, they promise.*

AH: Grief doesn't end. The ego's attachment to it can, however. In certain ways, grief expands on the spiritual path, but rather than being personal, it focuses on and embraces the grief of those around you. Part of the real meaning of spiritual life is to root yourself in such strength of silence and purity of love that you can open completely to the pain of others and help in their healing.

The way out of grief is not into another illusion but into the healing presence of the divine. Grief can be one of the most important purifying agents. One of the functions of the master is to make the ego's pain totally transparent to itself so that it longs with all its power to escape its prison. Unfortunately, many people who come to a divine master expect to be taken immediately into the realm of bliss. If the master is genuine, this is often the last thing that will happen. Instead, a series of crises will manifest in which all of the disciple's illusions will be revealed to them, sometimes with frightening speed and ferocity. You're made to face your responsibility for the film your darkness, rage and hunger are projecting. You are made to face the fact that the director of the film is deranged.

This is often the point at which people give up the spiritual life. Rather than getting the sudden fix of radiance they want, what they get is a mirror ruthlessly held up to their mask. This unsparing reflection is the prerequisite for the real journey. How can you begin to go out into the mountains of the Self unless you have faced the fact that all life on the plains is, in the end, limited and full of pain? How can you devote the stamina and ardor to the search unless you have come to the point of understanding that all other solutions but liberation are, as the Buddha said, like whitewashing a burning house? One of the primary reasons for going on the mystic journey now is to learn through endurance the strength necessary to bear what we and the rest of humankind have done to ourselves and to the earth. Letting the master burn down your house is the most frightening act of submission you can make and involves a heroic capacity for grief.

As Lewis Thompson says, "What is first necessary is exact experience of our Agony....Premature abandonment of Anguish is surrender of all real possibilities, lapses into Ennui, the incapacity to live. Evasion of Anguish is surrender to death, the inconclusive. The Christ completes his Agony."

Part of completing the agony entails the acceptance of another kind of grief, that which arises over the separation between you and the divine bliss you come to know if you open to prayer.

Once you've had a taste of the presence of the Beloved, felt the bliss that is your real Self and that of the master, there is born in the heart a great intensity of longing for perfection. This grief is in many ways the greatest and deepest of all.

But it is the Divine through the master that awakens this great flame of devouring grief in the heart, because only through it can what separates us from God be burnt away. Meeting God in a master is like meeting fire, and your task is to throw yourself into the flame. It's bound to be painful, but the difference between the grief you feel in the bafflement of illusion and the grief you feel in the immolation by the Divine is that the latter is fecund and the ground of a true life.

This process is perfectly described by St. John of the Cross's *Living Flame of Love*. St. John compares the soul to a log of wood, dank, dirty and covered with moss, that has to be first penetrated by fire and then consumed in it. The log cannot burn before its darkness is smoked out of it. St. John tells us that in this stage, which he calls the Preparatory State of Purgation, the flame is not bright to the soul, but dark "and it is not delectable to it, but arid, it brings with it neither refreshment nor peace but consumes and accuses it, neither is it glorious to it but rather makes it insidious and bitter." All mystics find this stage difficult and full of grief, but they know that the fire that is burning them is wounding them in order to heal them, and the death they're being taken to is a preparation for an infinitely wider life. This fire of love strips the log and enters it. Another kind of burning—of inmost love and ecstasy—now occurs. As St. John says, "for inasmuch as this flame is a flame of the Divine life, it wounds the soul with the tenderness of the life of God." When this tenderness is entered into, a strange and glorious amnesia begins, just as a woman after long childbirth forgets the pain in the beauty of her child. All mystics who have been through this process report great suffering but know that any amount of suffering is worth the sweetness of this birth into divine life.

MM: *I have been realizing more and more how important it is to accept your despair and to find it a friend. Instead of being frightened by your despair, you come to understand it as an extraordinary gauge of where you are. It keeps your sympathy alive. I've noticed that in a lot of so-called spiritual people, a very small progress makes them vain and makes them think that they have left the human race behind. The people I've met who've made great progress are aware of how deeply they share in the enterprise of others. That's the difference.*

AH: Yes. Opening to mystical life is opening to all the desolation of the world, containing it within oneself without any kind of fear or barrier. Especially when doing the yoga of the Mother, how could one escape from grief? The Mother is birthing this creation; to share her work is to share her pain. To love the Mother is to work humbly with all the darkness and difficulties of the world, to shirk nothing of the pain or opaqueness of matter and reality, to do the yoga of the Mother means facing unblinkingly what is going on in the devastation of the world, in the pollution, wars and torture chambers, to look with the Mother's eyes at a world eviscerating itself. Her yoga will ask you to confront every aspect of the agony of being. How can you heal a disease that you do not know completely? How can we hope to transform everything without facing everything?

When Martha and Mary came to Christ and said that Lazarus was dead, Christ wept, and out of that weeping came love and power that resurrected Lazarus. It is the response to the pain of the world, allowing the full tragedy of it to come in, that gives us the energy to work for change. What enables us to face the full horror without mitigation is the fact that the holy ones are here to help us, to show us that there is a real alternative which will not divorce us from grief but wed us more deeply to the grief of the heart of compassion.

As you grow in light and clarity, the pain of others becomes transparent to you. What you see quite clearly and without judgment are the marks of evasion, the wrinkles of desolation, and your heart is always open in love and grief for everyone. You learn to long for the powers that come with enlightenment, knowing that only those powers can be of any use in a situation as terminal as this. The illusions of what unenlightened action can do are permanently taken away.

MM: *Enlightened masters are able to absorb this grief and work without bitterness.*

AH: The Dalai Lama was once talking about what was happening in the world. He stopped and tears fell down his face. Normally, he is so controlled. People were very startled. And yet, in that moment, it was as if he had given us an insight into the furnace of his heart. The more deeply you understand emptiness, the more courage you can have in the dream.

MM: *Milarepa said, "Seeing emptiness, have compassion."*

AH: It's because Mother Teresa knows that the ultimate nature of reality is bliss that she can work twenty-two hours a day in situations most people would find intolerable. When Christ was faced with the choice of his incarnation, even he reeled at it. That's what you hear in Gethsemane, Christ coming to the end of the great drama and seeing what it would require to shift the axis of horror in the world—nothing less than dying like an animal on the cross. Even he said, "Lord take this cup from me," before finding the strength to say, "Not my will but your will"—the strength which led to the resurrection. It's heroism with a pain and love that no other life can begin to approximate.

MM: *But Andrew, you're talking about saints and avatars. What about the rest of us? How can we be inspired on the spiritual path by this terrible grief that we feel before illumination?*

AH: I'm not talking about grief in this way to discourage seekers. On the contrary, I'm trying to describe what depth, possibility, meaning I have found in grief. I'm so tired of versions of mystical life that play down this inevitable aspect of suffering. Nothing that I've said is exaggerated or morbid. This is what it's like. When you think of how much pain there is in life anyway, let us choose the suffering that leads to transformation. Let us accept the price, which is the grief of God and his love. Paradise is here but it can only be felt when all of mortality is embraced, when all of humanity has been gathered to you as brothers and sisters, when you live with the pain of truth and the love it requires.

Henry Suso, the great German mystic, once met a knight while crossing Lake Constance and was so moved by the knight's account of the dangers he had endured and by his stoicism that he swore never to complain again. When Suso arrived at his destination, however, the old distress returned. Then he had a vision. In it, the voice of his Self said to him, "What has become then of that noble chivalry? Who is this knight of straw, this rag-made man? It is not by making rash promises and drawing back when suffering comes, that men win the ring of eternity which you desire." Suso replied, "Alas, Lord, the tournaments in which one must suffer for you last such a long time." The voice replied, "But the reward, the honor and the ring which I give to my knights endure forever."

MM: *But as the ego is constructed to avoid pain, it's no surprise that it derides the mystical life which will open it to what it fears the most. Ironically, this unwillingness to grieve consciously and fully is a tremendous source of depression, a kind of living death.*

AH: In a world that makes suffering obscene, which tries to paper it over, our already developed ability to deny suffering is institutionalized. So much of the violence and vanity of our world comes from that hypocrisy. We're not taught to accept that suffering is a necessary prerequisite to growth. You ascend just as much as you have the power and courage to descend. As the Gita tells us: "What seems at first a cup of sorrow is found in the end immortal wine."

The alchemists knew this great secret—that if you did not bless and accept fully everything that was most painful and dark in you, you could never attain the conjunction of opposites, the sacred marriage, the philosopher's stone, because final wisdom can only flower from transformation of everything in the psyche, the bringing up into the light of spiritual consciousness and the releasing there of everything hidden in the dark depths of the unconscious. As Jung said: "One does not become enlightened by imagining figures of light, but by making the darkness conscious." This is necessarily a long, complex, sometimes painful process. How could so great a work be done quickly? And one of the paradoxes of this work is that we come to know our griefs as our most precious possessions. The very things we wish to avoid, reject and flee from turn out to be the *prima materia* from which all real growth comes. It is they who go on driving us into the arms of the light and they whose every corner of darkness will have to be illumined for us to be whole. So grief and healing work together and inspire each other.

Imagine what a flower goes through, what energy the seed needs
to endure the darkness in the ground all winter. Then it has to
break ground, survive the buffets of the winds of early spring and
allow the sunlight slowly to crack open its hardness. The reward
for that process, the opening of the flower to the light, comes
late and is hard earned. Why do we think that our kind of growth
is not going to be like that? The laws of growth and pain are
inseparable.

MM: *How is therapy useful as a path to this illumination?*

AH: It certainly can be useful, but it is very important to see its
limitations. I remember a Tibetan lama going into a peal of
laughter when someone suggested that even the Buddha
needed therapy. This is nonsense, a vain privileging of a minor
Western discovery.

MM: *That is very harsh.*

AH: The fact is that the Hinayana, Hindu, Sufi and alchemical
systems of thought are far more profound in their understanding
of psychology and full possibility of the human being than the
writings of Freud and Winnicott.

What we need is a completely new psychology, one which has as
its end not a decent sanity...

MM: *Freud's "manageable depression."*

AH: ...but a transfiguration of the being. What is possible is liberation, the sacred marriage, and any psychology which does not
have as its end the complete liberation of human beings from
the bounds of illusion is of limited value.

MM: *But is it appropriate to apply mysticism to the level of psychology? Ken*
        Wilber, among others, has pointed out that we are a spectrum of conscious-
        ness, in which different tools may be used for different purposes. I know
        many extremely neurotic meditators, for example, who rhapsodize about
        nirvana but cheat on their wives. It's easy to confuse this kind of talk, to skip
        steps and fall prey to spiritual bypassing.

AH: I agree completely. This can be very dangerous. Any real mystic
        progress, as I've said, involves continual facing of the shadow
        and the most unflinching, precise, exhausting work on the
        unconscious. The mystic is trying to allow the unconscious to
        become completely conscious. No corner of the life or mind
        goes unexamined. For all of life to be divinized, all of life has to
        be owned. This is a double movement of ascent and descent.
        The mystic has both to go continually into the light of the
        Absolute and to bring the light down into every aspect of his or
        her thoughts and actions. No aspect of grief, lust, rage, jealousy,
        envy or violence can be glossed over. For each of the so-called
        dark emotions has secrets to yield and trapped gold to liberate.

MM: *Rilke says that our deepest fears are like dragons guarding our deepest*
        treasures.

AH: Coming to know and harness the chaotic energy of our dragon
        involves the acceptance of a long and grueling process. As the
        alchemists taught us, many descents into the dark, what they
        call *nigredo*, and repeated burnings away, what they call *calcinatio*,
        of what is inessential, is necessary to this exploration.

        Freud, in his unconsoling analysis of childhood trauma, and
        Jung, with his precise understanding of the different steps of
        integration as well as his exploration of alchemy, can both be of
        great help. Both, however, fell short of the kind of all-embracing

mystical psychology that I see the future giving birth to. Wilber himself has been one of the most remarkable pioneers of this new transpersonal psychology which is still in its infancy.

MM: *How do you think this therapy will develop?*

AH: I believe that the West's infatuation with conventional forms of therapy will end in the same way the West's infatuation with Marxism has ended—in depression. We'll see the collapse of conventional Western therapy in the next twenty years. I hope that therapists will be required to spend more time on their own spiritual transformations. This will show them how inadequate are their current tools for understanding the mind. They simply don't know what the mind is, since many don't know the light that is shining through the mind. How can they understand what neurosis really is if they have no sense of how *samskaras*, the habitual tendencies of the ego, are created over many lifetimes? If they don't understand in some sense the transcendental nature of consciousness and have little knowledge of the workings of grace, how can they wisely and consciously help along the mysterious process of psychic healing?

What therapists are useful for is to keep people from committing suicide in a suicidal society. That is a valuable thing in a world as degraded as ours but has little to do with the final vision of what human beings could be.

MM: *In fact, the obsession with therapy can fix you in biography when the whole point of the journey is to integrate biography with the Self, the relative with the Absolute. Without an integration of these two dimensions, without an awareness of transcendence, no therapy can help us to freedom.*

AH: You cannot possibly understand the relative dimension without the absolute dimension. Most Western intellectual positions are merely dancing in the dark. Realizing this is what shattered my brain as a young man, realizing that most of Western psychology, philosophy and science are severely stunted. They have no understanding of the unconditioned and that vitiates many of their discoveries from the beginning. What sadder example of this could there be than Freud's description of mystical experience as a sort of regression into the womb and his denunciation of religious truth as evasion, when in fact both demand a ruthlessness of self-exposure that Freud himself resisted. Had I listened to the received wisdom of psychotherapy, I would have believed that all my visionary experience was psychotic. That would have set me back a lifetime.

MM: *Describe a therapy that would incorporate mystic awakening as its goal.*

AH: Let's call it divine therapy for humor's sake. It's point of departure would be belief in and knowledge of the superconscious, knowledge that our ultimate identity is eternal and divine, and that the end of therapy is to rescue our divinity from its unconscious state, free the gold of the divine spirit from the darkness of programmed, repressed and unconscious instinct. It would understand that the human mind is a reflection of the divine mind, the mind defined by the Buddha as "beyond mind." It would see the psychology of the ego not from within the ego but from the position of the divine witness, arrived at through sustained meditation. The witness, helped by the therapist, would take the patient into the seat from which he or she could watch the film and not be identified with it. Freudian therapy tells us that our identity is our traumas, memories and so forth, and that to understand this identity, you have to pick through the neurotic tangle. To a divine therapist, that would look like jumping into the cinema screen to rearrange the film.

MM: *Let's take this down from theory into nuts and bolts practice. I have pain. That pain arises in the mind that witnesses my relative self. How do I heal that pain in the transcendental therapy you're describing?*

AH: It's true that you have to heal the ego and the pain of childhood but from an awareness of the divine being. This is not at all easy, because one of the things that you discover during this process is that every time you make major progress, you will go through a period of depression, because everything in you that does not want the transformation will surface to try to claim you, all the doubts, habits, secret love of depression and enslavement. If a fox is caught in a trap, it will savage you if you try to release it. But if you wear strong gloves and go on putting your hand in the trap, slowly the fox will realize that you are trying to give it what it really wants, to be free. In the mystic quest, you have to be totally aware of how the ego will sabotage you but also of its longing for dissolution.

MM: *In other words, you have to heal the false identity with the real identity.*

AH: Rumi was once asked whom he saw standing before him. He laughed and said, "It is a long time since I have seen someone standing before me." He was saying that if you think you are looking at someone called Rumi, whose biography you know, you have missed the whole point, the sacred humor of this game.

That's the problem with therapy. When you're alone with a therapist, you're not usually alone with somebody who knows that they are also no one. Because most therapists preserve the fiction of their identity, they cannot help you go beyond yours. You can be helped only by somebody to the degree of his or her realization. Only a master is completely free in the end to take you to the place beyond personality.

MM: *Say more.*

AH: You say you are in pain. In order to illuminate the darkness of this pain, you must have a grasp on what has battered you. We are all trapped in the film that we take to be reality. This film is made by the false self, the ego. Through our lifelong identification with it, we insure for ourselves suffering and great mental distress. The only way to stop identifying with the film is to be helped by grace to enter more consciously the light that is projecting the film.

MM: *You have had this experience yourself?*

AH: Slowly, in meditation, I've come to be aware of two different people living my life. One is Andrew Harvey, who was abandoned as a child, who has known a great deal of repetitive disillusion and torment. The other person has no sex and no name, is the Self, is peaceful, confident and spacious. My task, like everyone's, is to learn slowly who this other person is and to allow this other person to come more and more into the forefront of my consciousness, to take over my senses, to illumine, purify, adjust and attune my motivations and actions.

Instead of being inside Andrew Harvey or Mark Matousek, you begin to be the person who is guiding, consoling, balancing those people, a kind of mother to yourself. This is a complex and mysterious process full of setbacks, but the healing that results from it goes far beyond what is envisaged by normal therapy. I see that what I'm slowly, and with many setbacks becoming, is the child of the Mother living a divine life in time, consciously, with a growing sense of wonder and humor.

14

HUMOR

Love raises the spirit above the sphere of reverence and worship into one of laughter and dalliance.

—Coventry Patmore

MM: *One of the dreariest things about the most traditional versions of spiritual life is their relentless high seriousness. God is much funnier than most people seem to think.*

AH: I have a friend who was doubting her master's presence in her life. She was four thousand miles away and said, "Look, if you really are authentic, I want a funny telephone call to cheer me up." Four minutes later, the phone rings. It was a person who hardly ever rings her, calling to invite her to an international pancake making festival ten miles away.

G. K. Chesterton used to say, "Angels can fly because they take themselves lightly." I've had so many examples in my own mystical education of the infinite playfulness of the divine power. It is endlessly bubbling wittily under our serious sur-faces. One of the functions of humor is to liberate this sense of wild sweet play. As it's said in the *Mirror of Simple Souls*, "love swims in the sea of joy; that is the sea of delight; the stream of divine influences." One of the proofs of a mystic awakening is that it brings with it a very developed, sweet, anarchic sense of humor. As Lewis Thompson says, "The deepest, the most subtle and complex and the most serious, can be achieved only as play—with the perfectly co-ordinated, perfectly focused and perfectly mobile detachment of play. In this it is one with Poetry and Divinity." Humor comes out of a radical knowledge of the stupidity of oppressive structures and concepts of all kinds, the hypocrisy of a world—and an ego—addicted to their definitions. Enlightened humor explodes those definitions from within, in order to outrage and flamboyantly derail them. The mystic uses laughter and a holy shamelessness as one of his or her most powerful weapons. People who've realized their divine identity know that they are entirely blessed by God in all their silliness and frivolity, and this releases them into the dance of humor, which heals and releases everyone around them.

MM: *There's an element of very great tenderness that comes with humor.*

AH: Yes. Foibles are forgiven; follies are celebrated. The hunchback and the pervert, the orange-lipped prostitute and the Brazilian transvestite are all welcomed to the feast; nobody is excluded. In that sense, humor prefigures something of the great feast of love that is the mystic's understanding, the great feast of forgiveness and tolerance that the Mother has spread for us in time. There's an element of deep humor in the way in which divine love embraces everything that strict society or the pious turns away from. Christ embraced prostitutes, thieves, even taxmen! All true masters have around them all sorts of people others think of as beyond any kind of pale, to add spice and grit to their play and to expose the disciples' lack of unconditional love to themselves!

MM: *This humor is often completely outrageous—camp almost—as you find in holy madmen such as Da Free John.*

AH: Absolutely. The person who has allowed him- or herself to cross all boundaries is beginning to enter the kingdom of unity which is sparkling with divine laughter. St. Teresa was once overheard singing a ditty about one of her greatest mystical experiences while sweeping the floor of the convent. Catherine of Genoa, than whom none was more exalted, occasionally refreshed herself with impromptu nursery rhymes. There are hundreds of stories about the lunatic aspects of Zen masters, of Nasruddin the mad Sufi, and of Jewish Hasids such as the Baal Shem Tov. This humor works like a sword to cut off the head of reason and reveal continually the presence in life of a power beyond anything as dull as "understanding."

MM: *I love the story of the Samurai who comes to visit the Zen master, Hakuin. The Samurai approaches the master and bows, asking, "Sir, I wish to understand the differences between heaven and hell." The Zen master looks at the Samurai and, eying him from head to toe, says, "I would tell you, but I doubt that you have the keenness of wit to understand." The Samurai pulls back in astonishment. "Do you know whom you are speaking to?" he huffs. "Not much," says the Zen master, "I really think you are probably too dull to understand." "What?" says the Samurai. "How can you talk to me like this?" "Oh, don't be silly," says the Zen master. "Who do you think you are? And that thing hanging by your waist. You call that a sword? It's more like a butter knife." The Samurai, becoming enraged, draws his sword and raises it over his head to strike the Zen master. "Ah," says the Zen master. "That is hell." The Samurai's eyes shine with recognition as he lowers and sheathes his sword. "And that," says the Zen master, "is heaven."*

AH: That's marvelous. You see that laughter explodes the ego in the way the most serious contemplation cannot. A person who is beginning to be free laughs in a full and magical way. I love what Anandamayi Ma says about laughter: "Your whole body must be united in laughter...you should shake with merriment from head to foot...I want you to laugh with your whole heart and soul, with all the breath of life...you will then see how the laughter that comes from such a heart defeats the world." Not only defeats the world but also transforms it, by revealing it for a moment as a field of enlightened play.

I am not being irreverent in saying that there's a humorous—even, as you say, an almost camp aspect to God. I'm trying to point to something that every mystic experiences, namely, the hilarious, dazzling connectedness of things. Synchronicity—the interrelation of signs and events like notes in a fugue of light—is a divine fact which has many comic aspects. Comedy has a serious purpose, which is constantly, wittily, to undermine and sabotage the fantasies of gloomy dread which the ego drags around. In one sense, life is an immense joke at our expense. Here we are thinking we are dying; in fact, being immortal. Here we are thinking we are trapped in a body; in fact, being a universe of light. Here we are thinking we are MM and AH; in fact, being souls traveling toward an ineffable union with God at some future Now. That's why Lonchempa, a great Buddhist Master, said that when you actually see what's going on, you nearly die of laughter. The Katha Upanishad says, "If the slayer thinks that he kills and if the slain thinks that he dies, neither knows the ways of truth. The Eternal in man cannot kill; the Eternal in man cannot die." Hidden in that sublimity is a vast calm laughter.

MM: *According to Hebrew tradition, God himself placed the humorous, way-*
ward or whimsical tendency in all people at the very beginning to prevent
humankind from "perishing from boredom."

AH: Ramana Maharshi said, "On the day of liberation, you will laugh,
        but what is on the day of laughter is also now." Part of the power
        of camp is to reveal, for a moment, a glimpse of that divine
        laughter that is constantly playing under everything. If the Hindu
        and Buddhist vision of experience is real, there is a way in which
        all of this is a fantastic, terrible and hilarious illusion, one which
        is kept going by our ego's constructions.

        Another power of humor vital to the journey is continually to
        make us aware of the doubleness of all things—that nothing is
        wholly good or wholly evil and that everything contains some-
        times saving and sometimes lethal contradictions. That
        doubleness is a very important part of understanding what is
        actually happening in this dimension. If you get lost in the
        tragedy of a situation, you will not see its potential for good. If
        you get lost in the good of a situation, you will not protect
        yourself from the potential dangers seeded in it. The humor of
        serene and canny detachment then becomes a source of
        protection and real freedom. The divine child laughs in the
        Mother's freedom from either good or evil. The Buddha smiles
        at the folly of an illusion which causes both so much pain and
        so much precarious unreal happiness. All dharmas are dream-
        like, the Tibetan masters say, and the best thing is to have a
        positive intention in the dream.

        Thinking of camp, could anything be campier than a Hindu
        temple, with its baroque proliferation of gods, its outrageous
        juxtaposition of realities, fellatio and divine meditation in
        opposite corners, a bull and Shiva, all forms of life dancing
        together in democratic and polyphonic perversity? This
        campiness contains a miraculous secret of freedom which has
        always inspired me and which many mystics in the Christian
        tradition (though, thank God, not all) seem to miss. Christ does

not do a great deal of laughing in the gospels, which is one reason why official Christianity has had such a sobering effect. I'm sure Christ did laugh, but it was edited out by all those ghastly early Christians. Holiness is *hilaritas* in the Christian sense, after all, lightness and joy. When people laugh happily, God is present. Mystical experience itself is a kind of laughter. One Christian mystic who saw this very clearly was Meister Eckhart who wrote: "When God laughs at the soul and the soul laughs back at God, the persons of the trinity are born. To speak in hyperbole, when the Father laughs to the Son and the Son laughs back to the Father, that laughter gives pleasure, that pleasure gives joy, that joy gives love, and love gives the persons (of the Trinity) in which the Holy Spirit is one."

MM: *Nobody who has been in the presence of the Dalai Lama could not know that laughter has divine power, the power of the Holy Spirit.*

AH: I was once in a group of people waiting to meet His Holiness at an airport in North America. Next to me was standing a black man shaking with pain and grief. When His Holiness passed, the black man took his hand and cradled his face against it. His Holiness took the black man's head onto his shoulder and leant his head very tenderly against it. Everything stopped while he cradled this man's head for about two minutes. Then he walked away, turned and laughed at the black man! It was a laugh of freedom. The laugh was saying, I have blessed your pain, but also remember that your pain is partly unreal. So, now, be free! The black man just stood there laughing also. Pain is passing, says Julian of Norwich; bliss is lasting. We will need to remember that as history darkens. Of course, we must be serious, focused, dedicated, impassioned, but we must also keep the springs of sacred laughter dancing in our hearts, otherwise tragedy will overwhelm and deaden us.

I think that one of the first things that happens in heaven is that God employs one of the campier angels to enact for you the more idiotic melodramas of your life, so that you laugh out forever any attachments to the ego which was that foolish.

MM: *We're so addicted to this idea of holiness as serious, but in fact humor and gnosis can be the same thing.*

AH: Catherine of Siena, although constantly sick, was described as always "jocund and of a happy spirit." St. Teresa was *"muy allegra."* Thomas à Kempis says of the lover of God "that he flies and runs and rejoices, is free and can be held by nothing." There was a famous saint at the beginning of the nineteenth century, the Curé d'Ars. He cured endless paralytics and sick people and was rather intense and severe in many ways. But every night his disciples discovered that he used to go to his church. They didn't know what he was doing there; they assumed he was praying or flagellating himself or crying out to Christ. One day they decided to follow him, and they found him lying on the floor in front of the altar laughing. Mother, give us all now the laughter of the Curé d'Ars.

Dante sees the whole universe laugh with delight as it glorifies God; the face of perfect love is adorned with smiles. In the tenth canto of the *Paradiso*, the souls of the great theologians dance to music and laughter in the heaven of the sun. Beatrice, as you would expect of the muse of the transcendent feminine, has *"occhi ridenti,"* laughing eyes, and laughs as she mounts with Dante the ladder of the stars. In the thirty-third Canto, perhaps the heart of his great mystical work, Dante talks of the light whose smile kindles the universe.

O *luce eterna, che sola in te sidi*

sola t'intendi, e, da te intelletta
ed intendente te, ami ed arridi.

Oh, light eternal, who only abides in
yourself, only yourself can comprehend
and, of yourself comprehended and yourself
comprehending, do love and smile.

MM: *It's the smile of bliss, love and wisdom.*

AH: And the smile that has been born in Dante's soul through
seeing *that* smile is the smile that knows that only the light is
finally real; that only God truly exists; that only love rules and
rules forever; that there is no death, whatever appearances to
the contrary; that evil is not absolute, but always swallowed up
finally in light; that what is mortal and transient is also
grounded in eternity.

As the great Tibetan master Dilgo Khyentse said, "Once you have
the View of the nature of reality...you will be like the sky; when a
rainbow appears in front of it, it's not particularly flattered, and
when the clouds appear, it's not particularly disappointed
either. There is a deep sense of contentment. You chuckle from
inside as you see the facade of samsara and nirvana; the View
will keep you constantly amused, with a little inner smile
bubbling away all the time."

On June 18, 1992, I was in Victoria Station in the afternoon,
about to take a train to Winchester. It was a drab, hot, humid
afternoon; the noise in the station was deafening; I felt myself
swim to the edge of panic. Then, quite suddenly, it happened. I
saw what I realized, with awe and gratitude, was the secret, the
root of that cosmic optimism all the masters have, of their

stamina and their, to the mind, outrageous hopefulness. I heard an inner voice say to me, "This is the intelligence of bliss." All the faces before me were in me, shining with the light. The old newspapers flapping on the floor were moving in celestial rhythm; the din was no longer menacing, but held and enclosed in a far deeper, ringing, silence.

The face swam before me in my soul's eye of a young multiple rapist I had spent an hour with in Pentonville the week before. As we had talked, I had seen the divine light on him, in him, and around him burning with a brilliance I had previously seen only around the Dalai Lama. I had been very surprised as we had been talking of the horror of what he had done, the guilt he felt, and the difficulty of wanting to go on living knowing he had inflicted so much suffering. In Victoria Station I saw his face again, but as if transformed, illumined, still recognizably his face, but irradiated now with wisdom. And I knew I was seeing him under the aspect of enlightenment, as he might look in the marvelous moments after the divine light had been born in his mind.

And with that vision, these words came to me. "Whatever evil is done, the essential nature of everyone, without exception, cannot ever, under any circumstances, finally be obscured or destroyed. Evil can create veil upon veil of darkness that it may take thousands of lifetimes to burn through but cannot finally obscure the eternal good in all." And I understood beyond understanding that it was this knowledge that had given Christ the power to forgive his murderers; that gives the Dalai Lama his astounding gentleness toward the Chinese; that gave hundreds of ordinary saints the power to die in peace and without hatred in the most horrible circumstances imaginable—in Dachau, in Cambodia, in the Gulags, in the Chinese concentration camps of

Tibet. This knowledge is the smile on the face of eternal gnosis and eternal love, the smile of ultimate humor.

MM: *Ultimate compassion.*

AH: And ultimate strength.

15

THE VISION OF LOVE

The earth and the sand are burning. Put your face on the burning sand and on the earth of the road, since all those who are wounded by love must have the imprint on their face, and the scar must be seen. Let the scar of the heart be seen, for by their scars are known the persons who are in the way of love.

—Mohammed

Love is the true means by which the world is enjoyed: our love to others and others' love to us. We ought therefore above all things to get acquainted with the nature of love. For love is the root and foundation of nature: love is the soul of life and crown of rewards.

—Traherne

MM: *Let's talk now about human love as it relates to the spiritual life. Many of us are able to sit in meditation, to read spiritual literature, to imagine the opening of our hearts, but when we come into intense emotional contact with other human beings, spiritual wisdom seems to go out the window. This leads to hypocrisy, confusion, isolation.*

AH: Ramakrishna said that he met his Lord in all the people that came to him. One clue to spiritualizing our relationships is to realize that everyone is a different facet of the diamond of God. The way to begin to understand that is to enter more and more deeply into communion with God and an understanding of what the Sufi and Hindu mystics call *unity*, which is knowing that everything in reality is reflecting everything else and is everything else.

This sounds grand, but as the mystic discipline deepens, this perception becomes more and more normal.

When you treat a relationship as a sacred meditation, a wholly new tenderness enters; a new scrupulousness and care informs the energy of the relationship. With that energy, the kinds of mistakes you might have been tempted to make before—of aggression, jealousy, demandingness—become much more difficult to make. Because your attention is focused on the essence of the other—and the ways in which opening to them brings up darkness in you that needs to be healed—you become increasingly unable to react in the old ways. You have a deepening sense of your conquest of your old self and its pain, which brings a great sense of joy and delight into the relationship.

This is a long process, requiring prayer and attention, but it is the great reward of the spiritual life. When you do not absent yourself from the world in some isolated or exalted way, you are able to enter completely into the world and to savor every encounter with every being as an encounter with the Beloved.

MM: *Unfortunately, the cult of romance teaches us to look at love as a frenzy of passionate sex, an escape from ourselves and the world, a drug to which we are encouraged to addict ourselves.*

AH: Cyril Connolly says that life without love is like an operation without anesthetic. That is a sad and unhelpful attitude toward love. Love is not an escape from anything, but an entry into a heightened dimension of awareness and responsibility in which the highest truths are at stake. This is a version of love that people shy away from. In a culture as hectically devoted to pleasure as ours, this vision is almost as threatening as the vision of enlightenment.

I believe that we are entering an era of spiritual marriage in which couples undertake to live together primarily for spiritual reasons. They will live together because in their pairing they find the balance, harmony and peace of body and soul they need to go forward. Children born from such unions will have much more integrated parents. Instead of placing an enormous emphasis on the relationship itself, lovers of this kind will use it as—or rather allow it to be—a discipline of the heart, a way of purifying their egotism. As Traherne said so beautifully: "Never was anything in this world loved too much, but many things have been loved in a false way: and all in too short a measure."

MM: *This has very little to do with what most people think of as love.*

AH: I know from my own experience that most of us have invented a fake theology of romantic love. Denied any transcendent outlet by this society, we have placed on romantic love the weight of redeeming our lives, of teaching us about the nature of reality, of enabling the kind of transcendence that can only be attained through prayer and spiritual communion with the Divine. Love has been made to bear loads and intensities it's not equipped to bear, and from that has come a great deal of misery. Romantic love is a wonderful but dangerous illusion, because it is most often a kind of idolatry. The other becomes the god at whose hands you receive grace or terror, and through whom you experience, in very dearly bought moments, kinds of ecstasy which are nearly always stained with suffering, rather than the ecstasy of the Divine which is free from pain.

The limitations of this pseudo-mysticism are well illustrated by a Sufi story. Shams I Tabriz, Rumi's master, met Kermani, a famous mystic who loved sex and claimed to see the divine beauty reflected in his lovers. Kermani said to Shams, "I see the moon reflected in the water." Shams said to him, "If you have not got a boil on your neck, why don't you look directly at the sky?" Every human being that you love *is* a reflection of the Divine, but it is dangerous to transfer your need for transcendence onto them. Love your lover not only for himself or herself, but in and for God, in and for the divine Self, as a shining of God, of the Self. The sexuality of such a union will be immensely softened and made more delightful and revelatory by a real spiritual communion.

MM: *It will, in fact, become a romance of the spirit.*

AH: Exactly. This kind of genuine romance always has the fragrance of the soul in it, a contemplative wonder at what is ungraspable and mysterious in the other. Two lovers with this awareness are not so much physically entangled as their souls are attempting to reach union through the body. This gives a heightened intensity and purity to the relationship, an urgency to communicate the depths of their hearts and their secrets. Genuine romance is an exchange on every level of all the depths that have been accumulated over a lifetime, the meeting of two whole beings who have constructed a rich spiritual identity for themselves and who come together with a passionate desire to share the treasures of their search.

MM: *This doesn't sound like a task for children. Rilke said, in fact, that love is very rarely for the young.*

AH: How can two people who've not yet constructed an identity know love? They fling themselves upon each other and break each other to pieces in an attempt to find some kind of clarity and unity. The love I'm speaking of takes years to understand and to practice. So much in the personality has to be made gentle or eliminated for a great power of love to be released. So many of the dark memories of childhood that block or deform our ability to love have to be unearthed, worked with and released.

The fruit of the spiritual life is that you can, in the end, love another being truly, both in the body and in the soul. To love consciously with your divine self another divine self is one of the highest experiences on the earth. To love consciously with your divine heart, which is boundless and boundlessly tender, another divine heart brings into the core of ordinary life something of what St. John of the Cross called "the tenderness of the life of God."

MM: *Yet many relationships continue to be based on convenience, finance and so on.*

AH: Can you really call them relationships? Who is relating to whom in those relationships? Can there be relationship when there is exploitation? One should be ruthless and say that relation begins only when clarity begins. Richard of St. Victor said that "to love is to see," and that demands of us a great effort of attention and imagination, a profound self-examination and the ability to *see* the other as sacred. What most people call relationship is the clashing of two ignorances, two catastrophes, two psyches in pain, as at the end of Matthew Arnold's "Dover

Beach," two "ignorant armies clashing by night." Hence the tragic suffering that we see all around us in our culture.

MM: *Commitment of the deepest order is essential to harmony.*

AH: Essential. But let us be clear about what commitment is. Commitment is the agreement of two mature people who have accepted that they are not immortal, that they do not have limitless reserves of time or endless options, and that the love that life has given them is something that they can work with only if they dedicate themselves to each other in the highest ways. The highest relationship of all, between master and disciple, cannot work unless there is absolute dedication. True love can only exist when two people are devoting a great deal of heart and concentration to it. It demands, in fact, the profoundest kind of commitment. You can't write a novel if you're writing nineteen short stories at the same time. Without commitment, there can be no final flowering or trust between two people. Many modern people accept in a sad, resigned way, the infidelity of their partner, for example, and take it for being the best that they can get. This is sad. When there is real trust, both people find reserves of tenderness and candor that they couldn't possibly uncover without that trust. They are able to feel that the other can receive their gift entirely and protect that gift with ardor and gentleness. If that ability to protect is not there, the gift cannot be given. People spend years with each other in half-misery trying to give half-gifts.

MM: *And suffering over sexuality. Why do you think that physical love can be such a painful component of this entire picture?*

AH: Because of passion and the vulnerability which fuels it. Most of us are trying to heal appalling wounds, quite mistakenly, by desire. Desire is blind. It is a physical, not a spiritual power, and often chooses for its objects other beings who have no real connection to us at all.

MM: *The minute the body is introduced between two people, the shadow seems to come into play.*

AH: When two people go to bed together, they have to be awake to the fact that they are now entering no man's land, a place where the darkest powers can disturb them, where they may be exposed to the saddest parts of their psyche. Of course, in this no man's land, miracles can take place. They can know depths and heights of intimacy which they would never have known had they not surrendered to each other. Unfortunately, it isn't often that two spiritually awake people do make love. If we were honest, most of us would say that we had truly made love very rarely in our lives.

As you grow in the spiritual path, you tend to want only the highest and the best. Not because you despise the animal side, not at all, but because you know where it can end up. You're tired of the various permutations of the plot, and you hold out then for the possibility of there being this other kind of rare encounter. What renunciation really means is giving up of lesser joys for greater ones.

MM: *Could it be that trying to spiritualize sexuality is trying to make it something that it fundamentally isn't?*

AH: Nothing is not spiritual. Sex by and for itself cannot lead to enlightenment. Nothing by and for itself can, not even prayer. Enlightenment is in a dimension beyond will. But sex *is* natural. And everything natural is spiritual and has spirit in it.

MM: *Even casual sex?*

AH: I don't think that what two people do can ever be completely
       casual. This idea of casualness is an inaccurate one. Once you
       understand just what is at stake in every encounter, the ex-
       changes of energy, the idea of casualness becomes impossible
       to sustain. It's terribly sad how people treat each other emotion-
       ally and sexually. So many seem not to be aware that every time
       you use and discard someone, you are creating a field of bad
       karma, you are deadening your heart, freezing your emotional
       responses and committing a crime against the sacredness of
       another being. This not only destroys your own capacity for love,
       but the pain can embitter the other person and lead them to be
       cruel to someone else. And so the wheel turns.

MM: *Until you acquire a wise and self-honoring self-control.*

AH: There is undoubtedly a time when a certain amount of control
       must be exercised. Socrates describes that reverently in the
       Phaedrus, where he describes the restraint that is necessary for
       attaining the higher levels of love. It can be painful and demand
       a kind of discipline that causes suffering and loneliness. This is
       unfashionable now, but there may be no way of achieving a
       spiritualized love, which can be sexual in the best sense, without
       going through a period of difficult control. It is helpful to face
       the fact that promiscuous desire, while not being wrong in itself,
       can be enormously distracting and can trap you in false relation-
       ships again and again. Having recognized that, you don't
       despise yourself for having these desires, but you treat them
       humorously and firmly and keep them in their place. Many
       people are trapped by sexual addiction, which brings them very
       little except brief, intense moments of pleasure which become
       increasingly similar. I look back at periods of my own promiscu-

ity without any disgust but with a very realistic sense of how little they brought.

MM: *Georg Feuerstein has called orgasm "the working man's version of bliss." Sex has become a low-level mysticism for many people, a search for ecstasy.*

AH: But there cannot be ecstasy without real love.

MM: *To learn this, periods of celibacy can be helpful. Unfortunately, celibacy is a misunderstood concept for many people. Rather than seeing it as a bridge to compassion for the* anawim—*the sick, the old, the loveless—as a tool for growth, it is too often viewed as a meaningless show of penance and self-deprivation.*

AH: Yes. *Celibacy* sounds a frozen word, but I don't think of celibacy as a frozen state at all, nor as an unsensuous one. True celibacy is being in a state of receptivity and of tenderness and of what Lewis Thompson calls "chastity," which is a feeling of very deep attention to others without wanting anything from them. The periods of celibacy I've most enjoyed have been when I was absolutely alert to the beauty of other people, able to appreciate that beauty, without being driven to desire it. It's a feeling of spaciousness, of joy, and it's often made me feel closer to people I might otherwise have been afraid to get close to. Celibacy can birth the gentlest forms of intimacy.

MM: *Yes, an intimacy which is tender, erotic even, but not actively sexual. This is hard to imagine, however, since we live in a pornographic culture in which the real Eros is hidden from us, even denied. This is one of the most terrible ways the "camp" controls us and keeps us depressed—through pornography and nihilism. How would the transformation of the sacred feminine affect this absence of real Eros in spiritual life?*

AH: Nietzsche said, "The Christians gave Eros poison. It did not die, but turned into vice." But not only the Christians are to blame. Every major religion has in practice denied or repressed the body and denied or repressed and risked perverting its sacred powers. I know of not a single sexually healthy society in the modern world. How can humankind be free to evolve to its full potential unless Eros is blessed, until its sacred feminine force of connection and revelation is restored to us in all its exuberant beauty?

Repression of Eros, as Nietzsche said, has led to vice and a worldwide epidemic of pornography. Pornography is a betrayal of the inherent spirit in every act, of what is essential, holy, and so thrilling about the human body. For centuries we have been force fed the coarsest images of desire. What would noble desire be like? In the atmosphere of real Eros, the entire being of the other is present, as is an extraordinary possibility, not only of sexual ecstasy but of an illumination of the heart, a religious illumination of that fire of desire that is forming and flaming through the entire creation. At this sublime level, Eros becomes one of the Mother's powers of initiation into the love that moves all things, a fiery tender revealer of all of the bonds that bind humankind together.

In his poem about the death of Freud, Auden writes, "One national voice is dumb. Weeping is Eros, builder of cities, and weeping anarchic Aphrodite." Eros is the force that draws a child to lie in its mother's lap, that invokes magical passion between lovers of all ages and sexes, the force that, in its highest manifestation, attracts soul to love, the soul of the disciple to the soul of the master, to be inspired by the holy fire of loving wisdom. Eros is a power of the *shakti*, the feminine power that springs from the source to form the creation; Eros is the child of

Aphrodite, the Mother in her splendor of love. Just as we have
betrayed, degraded and nearly destroyed the Mother, so we have
betrayed, degraded and nearly destroyed her child Eros. One of
the most wonderful effects of the restoration of the sacred
feminine to the heart of humankind will be the healing of the
world's sexual wounds, inflicted over millennia by body-hatred,
guilt and denial. And with that healing, new powers of generosity, fraternity and deep kindness will flood the world.

MM: *Yet Auden calls Aphrodite anarchic. That power in sexuality is terrifying for*
       many people. Isn't that savage dimension also an aspect of God, such as is
       found in Hindu art?

AH: It isn't savagery. If you look at the bas-reliefs of Khajuraho, you
       see every act explicitly portrayed but with dignity and calm.
       Khajuraho is revealing the world naked in bliss, beyond all
       judgment or morality, showing the shakti at play in everything.
       The paradox at the heart of tantric sexuality is that it is per-
       formed always with a tremendous sense of reverence and
       curbing of savagery. Ennobled sex is capable of abandonment,
       but always with a core of worship.

MM: *And allowing the shadow to play.*

AH: A spiritualized sexual relationship would have true abandon in it
       because two people are devoting their bodies to each other. In
       the Anglican marriage ceremony, man and woman say to each
       other, "With my body I thee worship." A spiritualized sexuality is
       not at all a sanitized one. Sexual abandon and spiritual intensity
       are not separate in the slightest in a love so great on all levels
       that fusion and its gnosis takes place. Only lovers who realize
       that sexuality is the physical grammar of the soul can reach that
       level. This sexuality is the highest human feast because the

heart, soul, mind and body are all present, all aflame and dancing in consort together.

Our current ideas of sexuality are probably as naive and limited as our idea of the physical universe. In a hundred years' time, quantum physics will seem elementary. If a spiritual revolution occurs, the vision of sexuality which emerges will make both our romantic and our orgiastic pornographic ideal seem absurd. As Teilhard de Chardin says, "Someday, after we have mastered the winds, the waves, the tides and gravity…we shall harness the energies of love. Then, for the second time in the history of the world, man will have discovered fire." There are powers in the body that can be unleashed by love which haven't yet been drawn on. In Nizami's masterpiece of mystical passion, *Leyla and Majnoun*, there is a moment when Majnoun sees Leyla at night across a lake, standing transfigured in the moonlight. He cannot move, his entire being becomes a flame of mystic joy. *Deep Throat* seems rather boring compared to that, don't you think?

St. John of the Cross says that when the fire of the Holy Spirit descends, it penetrates the body to the tip of the toes. When you realize that body and spirit are not separated, you begin to imagine the kind of human love that could be possible. It cannot be said too often that this vision is the opposite of—and end to—any patriarchal denial of the body, the opposite of disgust with the flesh. The transformation that the restoration of the sacred feminine brings is one rooted in acceptance, freedom from guilt, blessing of all things human. The Mother is saying to us all, I believe: "You cannot transform what you have not first blessed." Blessing the body and its desires enables you to begin to infuse those desires with light and to allow them to unfold into deeper and deeper kinds of love.

One of the essential tasks today for visionary artists is to try and imagine what this new love would be like, to experience it in their own lives and to create out of it. Such art would give to this battered and deformed world a real vision of what illumined, human love would be like so that people would have something to strive for, to give up their promiscuity for, to save the world for, knowing that something so marvelous can be lived in it. I think this is what Rimbaud meant when he said, "We must be absolutely modern: We must reinvent love." When you read Whitman's poetry to college students, the look of profound nostalgia, pain, and longing that comes into their faces is amazing. When these kids hear the sound of the true beauty possible between people, their whole soul yearns, and something marvelous flowers in that moment.

MM: *Organized religion doesn't exactly encourage this flowering.*

AH: Here again, our churches and temples have failed us. Imagine what our culture might have been like if the Church had shown us Christ not merely as a seer and judge but as a master of all the forms of human love carried to their highest most sacred intensity, and as an example of how we could live each of them with awareness and truth. A great Christ-energy of love, now twisted and darkened by denial, would have been released and our history very different.

MM: *Let us talk now about the role of sacred friendship in the transformation.*

AH: I believe that the light which the Divine Mother has brought down on the world is communicated heart to heart, friend to friend. I have noticed that the way in which the light is being spread is friend to friend. Two people who have intimate trust in one another talking of the deepest things, allowing their spiritual hunger to manifest, sharing her in simplicity. Because it is uncomplicated by desire, friendship has enormous power. At the highest level, the glory of friendship is that there is no domination in it; it is the free enchanted play of free beings, of free spirits. I notice that as I've made progress through the grace of the Mother, I've come to open far more subtly and gratefully to the wisdom of my friends. By learning how to listen to that wisdom, I find it constantly speaks to me the words that she wants me to hear.

MM: *True friendship is a spiritual partnership in which both parties vow to help each other forward.*

AH: During the period I describe in *Hidden Journey*, I came to understand just how revelatory friendship could be, through a relationship with a woman in her seventies in Paris, whom I shall call Astrid. She knew at every moment what I was going through because she'd been through a spiritual transformation under an Indian master. It had cost her marriage, and she understood exactly what its spiritual, emotional and physical price was. So, I was being watched over during each state of this opening by the light by someone who wanted, I knew, nothing less than my illumination. We often thought the same thoughts, dreamt the same dreams. I'd ring her, and Astrid would say exactly the words needed to take me into the next stage of my journey. I came to love her so simply that she became one of the sacred voices of my own spirit. All the barriers between us were translucent, so that we could quite naturally heal, instruct, inform and encourage each other. All this took place not in solemnity, but in an atmosphere of the sweetest hilarity, an atmosphere of the gentlest holy freedom.

I learned through my love for Astrid that when two beings are united in the mystical quest, the passion and joy of friendship deepen extraordinarily and open onto worlds of illumination. Two souls can play like dolphins in the transparent sea of divine love, cheering and inspiring each other infinitely. This wonderful form of friendship can be extended into small groups of spiritual friends, friends who sustain, encourage and inspire each others' quests. As Al-Hallat, the Sufi mystic, wrote, "Souls make cohorts: they form in groups according to their chosen affinities." In a time like this when history is dark and external society so materialistic, such "cohorts of souls" have an essential spiritual purpose to keep hearts aligned to each other in the highest sense and so to the heart of truth, the heart of light.

MM: *It seems to me that love in the service of illumination includes four classic paths of yoga*: Karma (*action*), Bhakti (*devotion*), Jnana (*knowledge*) *and* Raja (*discrimination*). *Would you agree?*

AH: I've never thought of it that way but I believe you're right.

Jnana yoga is not merely knowledge, but gnosis. When love has reached its core intensity, it becomes a form of divine knowledge. To know another being through adoration and service is to help open up those channels through which divine wisdom can be poured into you and to begin to understand the sacredness of the world. A Zen master gazing at a piece of grass sees the energy of the whole universe. William Blake, gazing on a piece of sand, saw the whole cosmos dancing in its energy. Socrates, looking at Alcibiades with the eyes of purified and sacred love, saw in Alcibiades a figure of the beauty that secretly ordered all the worlds. Jnana yoga uses love for its real purpose, which is to unveil the secret connection between all things.

One of the experiences that confirmed my vision of a sacred love happened when I was walking down one of the paths of the Seine with a young German I know after two days of deep communion. At the same moment, we both had the same mystical experience, of all reality becoming transparent like a Japanese silk screen and everything—the bridge, the river, the Quai d'Orsay with its great sundial—became transparent in light. Because we loved each other, we were seeing each other and the universe with the eyes of divine love, consciously and together. I had no idea that was possible, but it happened on a rainy cold December evening in Paris, and it confirmed my sense that there are whole kingdoms of love awaiting us if only we have the courage to enter them.

Regarding bhakti as a part of love's yoga, devotion means total surrender of yourself, giving up what the Tibetans call "self-cherishing." There is a marvelous Tibetan exercise called *Tonglen*, which means breathing all the pain, fear, doubt and ignorance of the other, in this case the lover, into your heart in the form of dark black smoke, and praying that it will destroy all parts of one's self-cherishing. When you breathe out, you imagine yourself as a wish-fulfilling jewel shedding cool light upon your beloved and giving him or her everything that is needed psychically and emotionally. This exercise would give lovers the opportunity to gaze deep into each other's soul—with all its sadness, imperfection and hunger for healing—taking on all that pain and being grateful for the chance of working for the other's liberation. If lovers and friends did that exercise together, they would come into extraordinary knowledge of the way in which the hidden Buddha nature can work in relationships. Love then becomes not just a personal experience, but a way of unlocking the heart to the whole world and to the shining of the divine mystery in everyone and everything.

MM: *And raja yoga?*

AH: In the context of love, raja yoga, or the yoga of discrimination,
       would perhaps mean being absolutely aware of any secret
       motivation that is trying to use this sacred love for your own
       purposes. We must be aware of anything in us which is trying
       secretly to work out a grief or a need or a hunger, or to exorcise
       past humiliation. Raja yoga is a commitment at every second to
       the most acute vigilance of the spirit. It requires a condition of
       complete candor with yourself, which can only be won through
       continual self-examination. In love, raja yoga is the sword that
       cuts away, again and again, clinging to any old bad habits that
       threaten the integrity of the new love; the fire of honor and
       conscience in which all traces of being mean-souled or grasping
       or treacherous are continually burned away.

MM: *And karma yoga would be lovers working daily for the well being of the other*
       in every dimension.

AH: It's very sad to me that many spiritual transformations have to
       be done alone in a time like this because so few people have
       this vision of love as karma yoga. If two solitudes could do what
       Rilke said—protect, border and salute each other—then the
       work of the journey can be done together. How strengthening it
       would be for seekers who were lovers to have each other stand-
       ing guard over their visionary selves, dragons guarding each
       other's deepest treasure, lions and lionesses circling and
       protecting the gold of each other's soul.

       The alchemists and certain schools of Mahayana Buddhism have
       claimed that final transformation cannot be attained without a
       partner and that human love at a high stage is the essential
       energy that prepares the ultimate perceptions. Human love

earths revelation and brings the divine experience down into all the ordinary details of life to reveal life's essential holiness, initiating both lovers in the process into the fullness of divine presence. As it is said in the eighth of the *Emerald Tablets*: "Ascend with great intelligence from earth to heaven and again descend to earth, and unite together the powers of higher things with lower things. Thus you will receive the glory of the whole world and darkness will fly about from you."

16

WORK

MM: *After love, work is probably the most challenging and time-consuming activity in human life. It is also, unfortunately, divorced from what we consider "sacred." This leads to a sad division in our lives.*

AH: The old separation between "God" and "the world" is obsolete. Our task is to integrate mystical awakening with full participation in the market place.

MM: *How else can the world be changed and saved? Love has to become active on every level. The depth of our current crisis is calling us to reimagine what transformative spiritual action and work must be.*

AH: The essential inspiration in this reenvisioning is the Mahayana Buddhist ideal of the bodhisattva, the being who out of supreme love gives up personal salvation in order to help all other beings toward liberation. Until everyone is free, a part of him or her will not be free. The bodhisattva's vast compassion is also a vast enlightened energy of service.

MM: *This energy of joyful service is what we all need now to be able to begin to address the immense problems everywhere of our world.*

AH: Without entering into the dimension of divine wisdom and love, we cannot be fed from the living and endless springs of divine power. Only being fed from those springs can make us strong or clear enough to do what we will have to do in the years to come, to endure what will happen and never, ever give up or be discouraged. To change the world, a great many of us are going to have to be both mystically awake and politically and practically active, and we will simply become battered or exhausted if we do not find the source of divine hope and energy in ourselves.

MM: *We see the tireless abandon you speak of in the lives of many saints and enlightened beings.*

AH: I love what St. Teresa said: "Do you suppose St. Paul hid himself to enjoy in peace spiritual consolations, and did nothing else? You know that on the contrary he never took a day's rest so far as we can learn, and worked at night in order to earn his bread...Oh, my sisters, how forgetful of her own ease, how careless of honors, should she be whose soul God chooses for his dwelling place. Works are the best proof that the favors which we receive have come from God....to give our lord a perfect hospitality, Mary and Martha must combine."

Richard of St. Victor in his magnificent *On the Four Stages of Intense Love* divided "the steep stairway of love" by which we travel to union into four steps: the betrothal, marriage, union or wedlock, and the fruition of the soul. In the first, the soul is awakened; in the second, on fire with love, the soul sees "the sun of righteousness," *sunyata* or Brahman. In the third, the soul passes beyond "significant" or "ecstatic" events and is initiated into the steady divine life. The soul "passes utterly into God and is glorified in him."

Most mystic diagrams end here, in this transformed union. But

Richard of St. Victor saw clearly that the marriage of the soul
and its origin could not be a barren ecstasy. In the fourth stage,
the soul—the bride—after being caught up into such final
delight, "is humiliated below herself"; accepts the pains and
duties of love after enjoying its sublimest raptures; and becomes a source, a "mother" of new life. The bride of God, the
sponsa dei, becomes the *mater divine gratiae*, the mother of divine
grace, a foundation of fertile, tender activity, a center of transcendental energy, a creator of spiritual families, and co-laborer
with God himself in the divine life. This is what our time is
calling us all to be: Mothers, fountains of radical confidence,
cocreators with her of a new world, cocreators possessing her
patience, humility, tenderness, tirelessness and calm.

MM: *To participate, in other words, in the complete nature of God the Mother—*
both transcendent and constantly active in love.

AH: Yes, and to dedicate all that we are and do, whatever it is and
wherever we are, selflessly to the Divine, to the Mother, so we
can become the instruments for her great work of transformation.
I try and keep these words of Krishna to Arjuna in the Gita always
fresh in my heart and try to live up to them: "Strive constantly to
serve the welfare of the world. By devotion to selfless work one
attains the supreme goal of life…performing all actions for my
sake, completely absorbed in the self and without expectations,
fight but stay free from the fever of the ego."

I have understood that the most blessed people in the world are
those like the Abbé Pierre, the Dalai Lama, Anandamayi Ma,
who know that the way to continual and true happiness is to
give your life away at every moment selflessly to God. The
happiest life of all is the one which is burning away consciously
in the fire of divine love and devotion.

I have come to see that karma yoga is the knowledge that to work with that consciousness of selfless offering is one essential key to the transformation. This kind of work has no stain of mournfulness or constriction on it. Who could be freer than Gandhi? Even as he was assassinated, he leaned forward and called his assassin by the name of God. He worked tirelessly as an agent of divine love, having given up all the fruits of action; giving them up to God freed him completely from all attachment to power or fame or even success. Such freedom can only be obtained by a holy abandon of the self. This has nothing to do with what the world ordinarily thinks of as renunciation. Our notion of abandon of self contains the ego as mournful spectator, which is exactly what true self-abandon does not have. True abandon is enacted in a state of serenity, bliss and joy. What the world needs now is hundreds of thousands of Gandhis willing to risk everything, calmly and cheerfully, to turn this terror around.

MM: *There's a wonderful story about Mother Teresa saying that people often express sadness that she's given up so many things, such as vacations and going to the movies. For what? To be the bride of Christ! Anandamayi Ma was once visited by a group of businessmen who prostrated themselves to her. She stopped them and began to prostrate herself, saying that they were the true renunciates, having given up peace of heart and the joy of serving the world in and for God.*

AH: Somebody once said to me that it's obvious that Mother Teresa is just a psychotic masochist. What is the ego's most powerful way of humiliating the idea of a religious person? By dismissing him or her as someone with a martyr complex, somebody indulging in a sick desire for self-punishment. That, of course, is how the ego protects itself from the full glory of the spiritual life. If it realized for a second the state of joy these people are in, it would die of chagrin.

MM: *Let's talk about the ground level fears of people in the area of work. Many people are caught between the desire for God and the desire for achievement. They fear that the drive which has defined them in a society based on work will be lost in the process of enlightenment.*

AH: Either you stay a slave of the work ethic or you begin to infuse your work with a sense of sacredness.

MM: *How?*

AH: There are laws. They're not at all easy—especially in a world like ours in which most work is alienating and boring—and everyone who begins this journey finds it hard for a long time and makes mistakes. The laws for the marriage of heart and mind and work are austere. Within each person's capacity to do so, beginning at whatever level you are, offer little by little whatever you do to God. Do *japa*, repeat in your heart the name of God, so that whatever you are doing becomes suffused with presence. I know shopgirls who do this, car mechanics, millionaire businessmen, actors, politicians. It works. Japa steadies, inspires, and reminds. Slowly, you will come to learn how to give up your purely personal will and share it with the Divine and let the Divine in you do your work and guide you. Slowly, too, a sense of peace and stillness will come as you release all clinging and anxiety.

MM: *As we realize our identity—and cease to identify so much with our professions—we will also release our anxiety over work and achievement.*

AH: And through that release, find a far richer, wider, happier energy, which paradoxically will allow us to do everything more efficiently.

MM: *Let us come back here to the Mother. One of the unique aspects of the teaching that the Mother seems to be giving to the world is her strong insistence that her devotees work in the world without spiritual elitism. The Mother is not interested in ashrams, in founding a movement for people who do not want to work, who want only to sit around and think about what they think is God. She wants people to be strong, self-reliant and unselfish, and to contribute to the world with whatever skills and gifts they have.*

AH: The path of the Mother is extremely testing because it destroys all categories, boundaries, snobberies, elitist separations. Cleaning the kitchen or mixing cement is as much a divine activity as writing a poem, and everything without exception is a part of God. Remembering this at all moments is what brings us into unity with her. This way of working demands the most extreme perseverance and stamina. It is easier to escape into the peace of a monastery or ashram than it is to live that peace in the center of life—but if you can, the peace becomes unshakable and life is transformed.

MM: *One problem in a culture that lacks a spiritual foundation is that work becomes yet another ersatz religion, or a means of transcendence, just like sex, drugs and rock and roll.*

AH: This is the major problem in a culture like ours which has no god except success. Work is made even more alienating by being made into the only way in which people can define themselves and achieve power over others. The intrinsic injustice of the workplace is exacerbated by that. It's a double bind; people are enslaved to work for the money to buy things they don't need that enslave them further, and they are enslaved to work to become "someone" and become "respected," losing in the process their real identity and authentic self-respect.

MM: *Spiritualizing work is the only way of turning these values around, however difficult it might be.*

AH: Spiritual life offers whole new dimensions of work. It gives a far richer picture of what true work is. In the Upanishads, it's said that the sage knows the action in inaction and the inaction in action.

People who've chosen the vow of the bodhisattva have chosen unending work, but as I've said, it's not felt as an imposition; it's known to be an opportunity for development, a source of joy. But there is a stiff price. To do such work, you need to have seen through your vanities, your false ambitions and undone the addiction to work. This might disturb and offend people at first, but it is the only way through. It is the intention, not merely the activity, that matters.

MM: *And the kindness you bring to it.*

AH: Unfortunately, our culture is split into a false leisure and a false work. This can only be healed by what the Mother is holding out to the world, one energy of love that sustains both and makes both a source of inspiration.

MM: *It's difficult to imagine this working in a world in which the majority of people work in situations where they're either exploited, bored out of their minds or both.*

AH: That is why our whole industrial system needs to be completely rethought. Keeping people slaves to its crazy belief in progress makes spiritual life very difficult and so frustrates the central purpose of life. There will always be difficult and dirty work to be done, but a wiser spiritual culture will wean people away from the selfishness and struggle for status which makes that work even more demeaning than necessary. I know tramps who are happier, clearer and more spiritually evolved than any of the millionaires or tycoons I know. Even in their poverty, they have kept alive a dignity of generosity, and it saves their lives.

MM: *What about "right livelihood"?*

AH: If you wish to help in the transformation, you must choose a profession which endangers your moral and spiritual growth as little as possible. You cannot be a spiritual seeker and sell weapons or indulge in racist politics. Your work must be subjected to the scrutiny of your spiritual knowledge. This will necessarily mean giving up the rewards of compromise, radically simplifying your needs and being prepared to live on little if necessary.

I know a millionaire banker who left his job when he realized that the only people who ever got to enjoy his swimming pool were his servants. What does the joy of life come from? It comes from love, art, prayer, the richness of the inner life. If your work deprives you of those things, stop it. If you want joy in your work, dedicate it and yourself to helping others.

MM: *Many people seem to want it both ways. They want inner peace without giving anything up.*

AH: They will never find peace that way. We must, as I've said, simplify our needs and find our real selves. That is the only way I can see of pursuing a spiritual life in this culture. What drives consumerism? Inner famine. People will cease to need so many things when they realize that they are the thing they need, when they possess their soul in patience and realize the peace and joy of the nature of mind.

This food of joy is what the saints and masters are here to teach people. Let us be honest. Industrial civilization is on the verge of collapse. The kinds of over-complicated lifestyles many of us have lived will have to adapt. Our form of industrial culture in fact has to adapt for the world to survive. Simplicity is freedom. Educating ourselves in radical simplicity is now the practical responsibility of every thinking person. What Krishna says to Arjuna is what we need to follow: "Every selfless act…is born from the…infinite Godhead. He is present in every act of service. All of life turns on this law…Whoever violates it, indulging his sense for his own pleasure and ignoring the needs of others, has wasted his life. But those who realize the Self are always satisfied. Having found the source of joy and fulfillment, they no longer seek happiness from the external world. They have nothing to gain or lose by any action; neither people nor things can affect their security."

MM: *Let us try to imagine what work could become again in a partially transformed world.*

AH: In the ancient world, every human activity was in principle a yoga, a means of union with the divine. Plowing and cooking, sowing, carpentry, weaving, building, poetry, philosophy, even war, were all seen as integral activities of the whole person, relating human beings to the universe and its laws. Since the Renaissance, this harmony has been lost. It is precisely this harmony in work that we as a race will have to recover for our lives to have any meaning. The masters are here to show us how to recover this and how to create in dedication to God a world in which it will again be possible. Most of what we have come to take for granted will have to be given up, and the whole basis of industrial civilization will have to be reformed, but the reward will be balance and a fresh natural spiritual joy in the work that is at the heart of every life. When people are truly dedicated to

God, there is no difference between action and prayer. And when there is no difference between action and prayer, we will be living, simply and normally, the divine life on earth.

17

SACRED ART

Veni creatur spiritus accende lumen sensibus infunde amorem cordibus.
Come creator-spirit, bring light to our senses, infuse our hearts with love.

—Medieval Latin Hymn

As I see it, the real function of the arts is to permeate the environment of the world with a metaphysical reality so that man is not alone with the ego.

—Cecil Collins

MM: *Your own work as an artist has been a search for a marriage between action and prayer. This hasn't always been easy, has it?*

AH: When I left Oxford in 1977 to spend a year in India, I had no idea what I was looking for. I was in a desperate state and felt that my art was not helping me but feeding off that desperation. I had been for years a worshiper at the shrines of irony and despair and had bought almost completely, even voluptuously, the Western romantic version of the artist as outcast and mocker at the false feast of bourgeois culture. My heroes were Pascal, Nietzsche and Kierkegaard. I revered Rilke but had hardly begun to understand him. What little spiritual sense I had was shy, confused and derivative.

I shall never forget the joy of reading Aurobindo's *The Future Poetry* one sun-dazzled morning on a bus from Pondicherry to Madras. I knew I was being spoken to by a completely fresh voice, by someone who knew the way out of the pit I had found myself in. What Aurobindo was telling me was that there was a higher consciousness possible on the earth than that even the greatest Western artists, like Shakespeare and Wordsworth, had achieved, and that the art of the future would be created from this mystic gnosis and make all the art of the past seem limited. For Aurobindo, the supreme achievements were not *King Lear* or "The Prelude"—revere them though he did—but the Gita and the Upanishads and the Rig Veda and the works of the Sanskrit poet Kalidas, for in them humankind was given, in words glowing with a high and serene spiritual passion, an accurate, complete, inspired and inspiring vision of its sacred identity and sacred destiny. Aurobindo paid tribute to everything in Western art that could echo such inspiration but made it clear—and how invigorating this was—that the greatest spiritual and artistic adventures were yet to come, that just as humankind stood at the threshold of another kind of being, so its art awaited a similar and astounding metamorphosis.

MM: A *second renaissance*?

AH: Exactly. But I had, at the time, very little idea of what Aurobindo meant by spiritual realization or by being directly inspired by the divine light or by dedicating one's will and ego absolutely to the transformation so that the Divine could use both as instruments of its love and perfection, but my whole being shook reading him. I felt I was being let out of a prison—a prison of desolation and depression, a prison of false adoration of false gods. And I understood that if my artistic life was to have any purpose at all, it would be in attempting to take up Aurobindo's frightening challenge—to put my whole being into the fire of spiritual transformation and make my art the servant of that fire.

MM: *Weren't you afraid of that commitment?*

AH: I was terrified. I knew how ignorant I was, how little spiritual wisdom I had. I realized that if I was to go on such an adventure, I could expect only incomprehension and derision from the world I came from, for whom "the East" or "spirituality" or "divine" were terms of foolishness, or worse. No one else in my generation that I knew had or even wanted to imagine such ideals. Aurobindo had revealed, too, that the Western tradition itself was inadequate as support and inspiration. I had loved the Romantics, for example, especially Blake and Shelley, but Aurobindo had made me see that the art of the future would have to go much further. It would have to begin at the level of awareness, of gnosis, which the Romantics and even Shakespeare only glimpsed, and it would have to spring from a very different artistic "ego," one that had been transfigured by mystic knowledge.

There were other fears also. Like most modern Western artists, my work had, as I said, fed off my grief and depression. I had grown attached to these as sources of creativity, and the thought of giving them up, and of giving up all the accepted "forms" they engendered, all the styles and genres, scared me. I had all the usual young man's fears, too, that I simply would not be good enough. But then I met my master when I was twenty-seven, about eight months after reading Aurobindo, and that, slowly, changed everything.

MM: *As well as reading Rumi for the first time?*

AH: Actually, I had been given Rumi in the Arberry translation by my tutor at Oxford when I was twenty-one. I was excited by the glory and extravagance of his work, but I had only the faintest idea of what it was about. I could see that Rumi was a wild lover of some kind, but what kind of love he was burning in, I had no idea. I thought the extravagance was metaphorical, operatic even, a kind of Persian indulgence. I had no idea at all then it was a natural outpouring of gnostic vision, the stammering of ecstasy.

But as I came into the presence of my master, I came also into the presence of Rumi and realized that he for me—far more than Shakespeare or even Herbert or Rilke—would be my guide, my master in art, one of my spiritual masters in fact, although not in a body.

Rumi realized for me completely Aurobindo's vision of what a sacred artist is. Before he met Shams I Tabriz in 1344, Rumi had been a theologian, an intellectual. His spiritual passion for Shams and the splendor and agony of their love for each other transformed him into perhaps the world's greatest mystical poet. He knew and was what he sang; there was no dissonance between his life and his work. He became the fire itself, and all his greatest poems are living flames of that fire. Read in a state of true receptivity, his poems are direct sacred transmissions. Of all the enlightened beings who have left artistic memorials of their enlightenment—I think of Hildegard of Bingen, St. John of the Cross and Ruysbroeck in the Western tradition; Vyasa, Tsongkhapa and Basho in the Eastern—Rumi is for me the most completely inspired.

When, as will happen in the next phase of human evolution, Western ideas of genius are revised and the great mystics and sacred artists are restored to their rightful position at the center of all achievement, Rumi, along with Lao Tzu, the Mahayana masters, St. John of the Cross and the masters of medieval polyphony, will seem far more crucial than Shakespeare or Wagner or Nietzsche. Through Rumi, divine love speaks directly to the heart of the human race to awaken it to its secret glory and the glory of God, what the Sufi masters call *kibriya*. Many of his greatest odes he signed "the silent one," meaning that it was Shams who had really written them, not him, and this for me was a great clue.

MM: *A clue to what?*

AH: To the relation of the sacred artist to the Divine. What the mystic comes to learn is that God (or the master, who is God on earth, as Shams was to Rumi) is the supreme, the ultimate artist, the only real creator, and the universe is the unmatchable master-piece. "God is beauty," says the Koran, and all beauty comes from God, from the Beloved. Stand on a beach and watch the gigantic play of lightning in the sky and on the sea, and all art pales. Watch the sun explode into a thousand soft reds at sunset over the Himalayas, and the most glorious poem be-comes a faint memory. Enter into the bliss of presence, and even the deepest pleasure of the mind, even the most extreme, most refined aesthetic delight are as nothing, straws in a vast bonfire. Rumi cries, "The sun is risen! In its vast dazzle every lamp is drowned." "One hour of love is worth a hundred worlds." "Language is just a handful of dust/a breath of His blows away."

MM: *Then why create at all?*

AH: Out of adoration, awe, love, gratitude. Out of a spontaneous ecstasy, sometimes as Rumi did, possessed suddenly by love itself. Out of a desire to break the bread of rapture and wonder with others. Out of all these linked, sacred emotions, and in a state of surrender. You cannot fake this state; you have to be burned away, again and again, to come into its grace. It costs, and has to cost, everything. Divine love, as Rumi said, cannot be handed over like a stone. To become an instrument for the Divine to use demands death after death. It can be very dangerous for someone on the mystic path to want to remain an artist, unless you dedicate your art continually to the Divine.

MM: *Because the artistic passion reinforces the ego.*

AH: Yes. The ego will try to appropriate the experience or fake a minor crisis or two, so as not to have to go through the real burning. Chaliapin said to Gorky, "My life has as its leitmotif the struggle against the sham glitter that eclipses the inner light, the complexities that kill simplicity, and the vulgar externals that diminish true grandeur." Every real artist, whether mystic or not, fights this essential fight—especially in our time when sham glitter, complexities and vulgar externals are adored and rewarded on a universally degrading scale. But for the mystic artist who knows that salvation and liberation are at stake, this fight is even more exacting. Only the greatest possible love of God and a continual discipline of humility can save the mystic, who is an artist, from the dangers of inflation. What would it profit a mystic poet if he or she won the Nobel prize and lost that burning of the heart that Rumi knows "is everything, more precious than the empire of the world, because it calls God secretly in the night"?

MM: *How is this dedication possible without a master?*

AH: The master need not be in the body, but there's no doubt that devotion is the only love strong enough to draw the artist away from the intoxicating image of self as creator, toward work as the sacred child of a force infinitely greater than any human creator. The artist has an ego at least as strong as a businessperson or soldier or lawyer, stronger in some ways and, in many ways, subtler. To make the transition from fake master to instrument of God demands, as I have said, death after death. For myself, I could not endure this process if I did not love the Mother with all my heart and mind and soul, and if I did not know that whatever happens, happens to guide me forward into the truth she wants to give me. Not only could I not endure the process, I would be continually waylaid if I was not with her and constantly looking into the highly unflattering mirror her beauty and simplicity are always putting up to me; waylaid by my vanity, hypocrisy, hunger for celebrity, by unconscious motives and fears and ancient miseries, waylaid by the power that words and images themselves have to divert one from the austerity of the truth. Knowing and loving her, I know that only the enlightened live always in the kingdom of true poetry, that only they are the real artists, being artists at every moment in every dimension of divine love and divine truth. As Lewis Thompson wrote, "Christ, supreme Poet, lived truth so passionately that every gesture of his, at once pure Act and perfect symbol, embodied the transcendent. Baffling like blinding light is this command of form."

I have come to know the Mother as the supreme poet and the power of her grace as the most beautiful of all arts, fantastically and fabulously beautiful in its games and dances of transformation. Anything I write or say could only ever be at best a small and inevitably cracked reflection of this glory that will always transcend anything that is or can be said about it.

MM: *And if the artist is really working to reflect his or her reverence for the Beloved—however imperfectly—it won't be the artist as such who is creating.*

AH: Ramakrishna tells a wonderful story to illustrate this. The writer of a hymn to Shiva felt proud of his achievement, but his pride was dashed to pieces when (in a dream) Shiva's bull bared his teeth. He saw that each tooth was a word of the hymn; the words had existed from the beginningless past. The writer had only discovered them.

I had countless humbling and hilarious experiences like this when writing *Hidden Journey*. I would write a passage, and a few hours later, the Mother would repeat by a phrase or a gesture something I thought I had invented by myself, as if to show me who was really writing the book. Anyone who is brought by grace to create in the light will be sustained by echoes and games and synchronicities, by signs that reality itself is participating in the work. They will also be reminded in this way who is the real creator and from where whatever they are able to transmit is streaming. It is a marvelous game, one the master has already won in eternity and for eternity, thank God.

MM: *Let's backtrack a bit. What did you learn about the making of sacred art in the process of writing* Journey in Ladakh *and* Hidden Journey?

AH: *Ladakh* came out of a continual meditation on Thuksey Rinpoche. I would have to create the Rinpoche's atmosphere in my room and in my heart before I could begin to write. I'd have to imagine myself, sitting in Oxford, in the light-filled crevices of the Karakoram Mountains. I'd have to reconstruct the smell of the Ladakhi mornings, of Tibetan incense in the chambers, of lavender, of the rain on the mountains, of his wonderful small room in which he sat. There were many times when I actively felt the Rinpoche's presence in the room. I'd be walking up to write the book in the early morning in All Souls, and the light falling would seem to have the color of his gold robe. I would have to stop, because the bliss being sent to me was so great that I could not move. Slowly, I found the secret for myself of sacred art, which is to steep myself totally in sacred love and to write from that and from gratitude.

MM: *And in writing in this spirit and with this motivation, you really began to learn what he had to teach you? In other words, the transmission the Rinpoche had begun to give you in Ladakh was completed by the act of attempting to write about him?*

AH: Yes. Meditating on him, on everything he was and said, took me deeper and deeper into him. I began to learn that by thinking passionately of an enlightened master like him at every moment, you could begin to enter his wisdom mind, and your own, and receive guidance and inspiration from his dimension. And realizing this, I realized the truth of what the Rinpoche had told me in Ladakh when I had explained to him my fears of ceasing to be an artist if I took up the spiritual path. I told him a story from Kafka about a monk with a beautiful voice. One day, a holy man came to the monastery where the man was and heard him sing. He said, "This is not the voice of a man; this is the voice of the devil," and immediately in front of all the monastery, he exorcised the monk, who collapsed into a writhing, stinking heap. The monk was nothing without his voice, and its intensity and sweetness came from evil. After I told the Rinpoche this story, which revealed clearly my fears about my art, its sources and my attachment to them, he replied, "It is good that you know that you must change…that you must no longer work from anger or bitterness or pride….But it would not be good if you came to believe that there was no work possible that was not evil….The story you told me is moving, but it is only partially true. It is stupid to imagine that Evil has the sweetest music. The most beautiful paintings and sculpture, the greatest poetry, have sprung from contemplation, from joy, from compassion. You need to strive for a new relationship with your work. With time and sincerity, you will discover a way to work and write that does not harm you spiritually. You will find a voice that is not your voice only. If you can be humble enough, that voice can inhabit and use you."

In writing the book, I began to discover the truth of what he meant. That was his blessing to me and the blessing of the process of writing it.

MM: *Writing* Hidden Journey *must have intensified this process manyfold.*

AH: The difference between the books is, for me, very great. One is an account of the ego beginning to open, and the other is an account of it breaking apart and discovering a completely new, chaotic, vibrant divine world.

In *Hidden Journey*, I had to write a book which would reconstruct as scientifically as possible the stages of a mystical explosion in the light of the Mother, to give a map of that to anyone who needed or wanted it. That was my task, and it could not be a more frightening one. There was no precedent for it that I knew of. I had to start with total trust of the Mother. That meant that I had to give up all my vanity as a writer and a mind. I had to say inwardly to her, I do not know how to write this book, whether it can be written. Only you can teach me. I had to give up my will to her, at every moment, so completely that she could guide me from insight to insight, dream to dream, effort to effort, until I found— was given—the voice and structure. I had to follow each stage of the initiation with surrender, or else nothing could take place.

I also found very early on that I could not write anything except when I was in deep communion with the Mother. I needed to enter a particular state which happens in the mystic heart, of advanced absorption, soaking in the light which becomes present. That was the only state in which words were allowed to come.

MM: *I doubt that the lessons ended when you finished the manuscript.*

AH: Hardly. Three deaths were necessary for the process represented by the book to be complete: first, the partial mystical death into her; then the long, exhausting, beautiful death of trying to write about it; then the death of any attachment, either to the experience itself or the work that came out of it. That was in some ways the most difficult death of all. The miracle is that through her love and the growing calm, security, joy and health it brings me, each of these deaths is long ago forgotten, seem now to have happened to someone else. Whatever fears or griefs are endured on the journey in her will always be dissolved in joy; whatever wounds you sustain in the service of the Divine will always be healed by the "peace that passes all understanding." The Andrew Harvey that wrote *Hidden Journey* is long gone, and someone else, lighter, and more confident and childlike, is living in his skin. And this is all her work, not mine, her gift, her grace. And so all artistic "biography" is dissolved in wonder and that wonder brings peace, the beginning of freedom at last from a long fantasy of being the doer, the actor, the writer. This healing is recent and astonishing, and I am stumbling a little in its happiness.

MM: *So the sacred artist comes to feel anonymous?*

AH: Much of the greatest sacred art of the world has been done by those who did not sign their name. Who wrote the Rig Veda or

the Upanishads or the marvelous Latin hymns of the early
Church? We do not know who carved the saints at Chartres or
who sculpted the reclining Buddha at Pollunaruwa. The archi-
tects of most of the miraculous temples of Pagan in Burma are
unknown. Those who painted the leaping, flickering animals of
Lascaux left no name.

Perhaps the real question is not whether you sign your work but
whether you really let yourself become inwardly anonymous, an
empty space to be filled by the Divine. In this sense, Cezanne is
anonymous, and so is Brancusi. So are Basho and Onono-
komachi and Hadjewich of Antwerp. All have become, in
Hildegard of Bingen's phrase, through long years of ardor and
surrender, "feathers on the breath of God," and their work shows
it. In the last Cezanne landscapes, the whole of reality is suffused with a secret light and trembles in just that hidden fire of
shakti that I saw when I first saw Arunachala and was graced with
the vision of the sacred energy of the universe permeating and
emanating everything.

I remember walking into a New York gallery and seeing a group
of Brancusi sculptures, and they all glowed, really, with divine
light. Basho's greatest haikus are unmistakable telegrams, as
Emily Dickinson's poems are, from the enlightened mind. In
each case, *kenosis*, emptying out, has happened, and the Divine is
directly present. Furtwangler used to say that he did not dare
conduct Beethoven's *Missa Solemnis* too often because the holy
ghost was so active in its splendor and passion that he did not
know if he would survive it. Simone Weil used to "hear" the
breath of Christ and the humility of divine tenderness in the rise
and fall of Gregorian chant. I hear the creation singing in ecstasy
in Tallis's forty-part motet *Spem in Alium*. It is clear if you know
the rest of Tallis's music, which is wonderful enough but not at

this level of sublimity, that it was in this motet alone that "Tallis" vanished and his angel, his Self if you like, the divine person in him, could receive and transmit completely divine dictation. When art is created in this dimension, it takes on direct initiatory power.

MM: *The art you envision for the future will require such power as a standard of excellence?*

AH: I believe that the art that could forge, sustain and inspire the future will be made by mystics directed by divine masters in this sacred inner anonymity, this inhabited emptiness, for the glory of God and the evolution of a new humankind. There are many, many modern artists now, like myself, consecrating their art to the Divine in different paths, and as the tremendous beauty and power of what is possible becomes more and more accessible to people, and as people grow more and more exhausted with the pathological pablum and trivia they are being fed—and they will—there will be many more. Part of the gift of the restored Divine Feminine will, I am sure, be a flood of mystic creativity in all the arts and sciences. If we survive the next crucial, danger- ous period, if we really make the choices we need to make, I am certain a second renaissance far more important and trans- formatory than the one that flowered in the fourteenth and fifteenth centuries will be possible. Look at what is available now to us. Most of the great texts of the mystical traditions are in translation; all the media are amazingly developed. Think what could be done in film, in music, in poetry, to inspire and ennoble if there could be a change of heart and direction. The light is here; the means are here; now *we* have to be here, have to be present, passionate enough to give ourselves over to that light that is longing to transfigure us and be willing to die and die again into fresh creativity.

MM: *This second Renaissance could be further-reaching, even, than the first.*

AH: Yes, because this time it will not be rooted in mental pride, a
flight from God, a separation from nature, but in a great movement of return, return to the Mother, the earth, return to the
soul. In the apocryphal *Hymns of Jesus*, Christ, standing in the
center of a circle of disciples, says, "I am the word that plays and
dances all things…now answer to my dancing and understand
by dancing what I do." Blake speaks for the sacred makers to
come when he says in "Jerusalem":

> I rest not upon my great task
> To open the external worlds, to open
> > the immortal eyes
> Of man inwards into the worlds of thought:
> > into eternity
> Ever expanding in the bosom of God, the
> > human imagination,
> O saviour, pour upon me thy spirit of
> > meekness and love
> Annihilate the selfhood in me; be
> > Thou all my life.

And for this task what is needful? asks the Taittiriya Upanishad
and answers itself:

> Righteousness, and sacred learning and teaching
> Truth, and sacred learning and teaching
> Meditation, and sacred learning and teaching
> Self-control, and sacred learning and teaching
> Peace, and sacred learning and teaching
> Ritual, and sacred learning and teaching
> Humanity, and sacred learning and teaching.

To survive what is to come, we, as a race, will have to summon
up our utmost powers of passion, love and celebration, and if we
do, our arts and sciences will become what they have been
before in marvelous moments in China, India, Egypt, the Middle
Ages—the dancing grounds of the gods and of the Divine in us.

18

ADORATION

> We always make offerings to the sun
> And to the mountains
> And to the stars.
> That is why we live here.

—The Kogis

The cup in which the world is reflected is the heart of the perfect man. That mirror that shows reality is the heart. The heart is the treasure of the divine mysteries. Ask the heart, then, what is the purpose of the two worlds.

—Lahiji

Every visible and invisible creature is a theophany or appearance of God.

—Erigena

God wants the heart.

—Talmud

> He held me to his chest
> And taught me a sweet science.
> Instantly I yielded all

I had—keeping nothing—
and promised then to be his bride.

I gave my soul to him
and all the things I owned were his.
I have no flock to tend
nor any other trade
and my one ministry is love.

If I am no longer seen
following sheep about the hills,
say that I am lost, that
wandering in love I let
myself be lost and then was won.

—St. John of the Cross

MM: We've talked about spiritual discipline, the acceptance of grief, love and laughter, which take the seeker of God a long way toward his or her goal. But isn't it true that until we elevate those feelings to the level of adoration, we will not know the full mystic experience or come into the full presence of the Mother?

AH: Yes, but let us be clear about what adoration is. Adoration is not some fervent spiritual or poetic exercise reserved for a chosen few. I believe the human race will die out and destroy nature if it does not learn again how to adore God, the God in all of us, God shining and living in nature, and learn again how to act from and in that spirit of adoration. Adoration is nothing less than the oxygen of survival, the way itself to that illumination that alone can give us either the knowledge or the courage to save ourselves and nature now. As Abbé Pierre says, "In the struggle against evil and disaster, adoration is the ultimate help."

There is a worldwide famine of adoration, and we are all visibly dying in it. The desolation, nihilism, meaninglessness, tragic and brutal carelessness and perversity we see all around us and in us is the direct result of living in a spiritual concentration camp in which we are starved, and have starved ourselves, of just that food our hearts, minds and souls need most—the food of worship, of love, of gratitude, of praise, the bread and the wine of adoration. We have forgotten how to renew ourselves in the fire and the light of the simple, divine glory of life itself and forgotten how to know that joy and light in us and around us that initiates and heals all who realize them and gives sacred fire to all true action.

Adoration is both the way home and home itself, the sign and seal of true knowledge and the path to it, the radiant summit of the mountain of God and the force that gives the passion, the heart, the energy to scale it.

MM: *Allah says in the Koran, "I have only created man to adore me. I was a hidden treasure and wanted to be known. This is why I created the world."*

AH: And he adds in a *hadith,* "My sky and my earth cannot contain me but I am contained entirely in the heart of he who adores me." Why are we here? We are here to learn through adoration that "love that moves the earth and the stars." Coming to know that love and its shining in all things opens our heart more and more to it in an ecstasy of tenderness and gratitude until that time comes when all the sinews of our heart have been eased back and opened so wide that this entire universe and our entire experience in it can be placed within. This is the nirvana of the Buddhists, the moksha of the Hindus, the sacred state of "oneness" of the Kogis and the Yamomomis and Aborigines. This is the shattering of the cage of time, of life and death.

Constant adoration is the one force nuclear enough in its intensity to do this great work. As Traherne said, "You never enjoy the world aright till the sea floweth in your veins, till you are clothed with the heavens and crowned with the stars; and you perceive yourself to be the sole heir of the whole world, and more than so, because men are in it who are every one sole heirs as well as you." And coming to "enjoy aright" you, in the words of the Isa Upanishad, "behold the whole universe shining in the glory of God," and know what the Navaho Indians knew who created a magnificent night chant to the Divine Mother:

> I am walking with dark clouds
> I am walking with spring rain
> I am walking with leaves and flowers
> I am walking on a trail of golden pollen
> May everything be beautiful below me
> May everything around me be beautiful
> It is begun in beauty
> It is finished in beauty.

MM: *As you describe it then, this state of oneness through adoration with the universe is not static, but participates in the dynamic wildness of the universe itself and of God.*

AH: Yes, the enlightened heart-mind is not only rooted in peace; it is expanding as the external universe is, at the speed of a light that travels infinitely faster than its physical equivalent. Into a heart constantly widened by the power and bliss of adoration can be poured endless light, love and knowledge in continually expanding spirals of intensity and energy, an intensity and energy that have no end in any dimension, as Gregory of Nyssa and Rumi and the Mahayana mystics and Aurobindo all knew, because God and infinity have no end. Adoration is the *shakti*, and its work in us and all things, the sacred power of the Mother, is taking up everything in the universe to some immeasurable and unimaginable consummation in her.

MM: *Some mystics have beautifully suggested that this adoration of God's gifts actually increases God's delight in the creation.*

AH: The spiraling upward and ecstatic movement of adoration I have been trying to describe is all happening within the mystery of God and is part of the inexpressible beauty of that mystery. Why should our praise of God and his gifts also not deepen the Divine's own joy in creation, since we are part of the Divine growing in the Divine? Traherne expresses this perception perfectly:

> *Thy soul, O God, doth prize*
> *the seas, the earth, our souls, the skies;*
> *as we return the same to thee*
> *they more delight thine eyes*
> *and sweeter be*
> *as unto thee we offer up the same*
> *then as to us from thee as first they came.*

Through adoration, we coparticipate, cocreate ourselves with God, allowing God to grow in us. How could this not expand God's own joy? All mystics have felt in their deepest being the rapture of the Divine's response to their outfolding into love, just as the prodigal son did when he saw with wonder his father running out of the house and down the road to greet him and fold him in his arms. How amazing it is that each of us has in his or her power the ability to move God with such joy.

MM: *Your vision of adoration is sublime, but how can it affect our daily lives?*

AH: I don't think any of us begins to see what daily life is until we
grow in adoration. To grow in adoration means to grow eyes of
wisdom, eyes of love, the eyes of the Mother. Everything,
absolutely everything, is changed beyond recognition by this
deepening seeing. Cleaning your teeth is different, cooking is
different, washing up is different, going to the toilet is different.
You come to start to know the joy and peace Brother Lawrence
knew in the bustle of his noisy kitchen and what Julian of
Norwich meant when she said that God serves us in all things,
"even in the lowliest of our bodily functions." Adoration dissolves the madness of the separation between "sacred" and
"profane" which exists only in our imagination, ends pseudo-
judgment, pseudo-reason, derails forever the tyranny of
Newton's "single sleep." The ordinary world is revealed for the
brimming glory it is. Having a bath becomes prayer; sharing a
beer with an old friend becomes prayer. Cheap songs on the taxi
radio in the rain send essential mystic messages; the Mother
sings and dances and claps her hands in everything, in the
bedraggled geraniums along the cafe balcony as much and as
"holily" as in the most sublime sloka of the Gita. Everything is
sign, signal, spark, secret laughter. This is madness to the
ordinary mind, but what on earth does the ordinary mind know?

MM: *Ramakrishna said, "When you are intoxicated with Divine love, you see God
in all beings."*

AH: He also said, "The Gopis see Krishna in everything: to them the
whole world is filled with Krishna. They said that they themselves were Krishna. Looking at the trees, they said, 'These are
hermits absorbed in meditation on Krishna.' Looking at the
grass, they said, 'The hair of the earth is standing on end at the
touch of Krishna.'" He also tells us, "I used to worship the deity
in the Kali temple. It was suddenly revealed to me that every-

thing is pure spirit. The utensils of worship, the altar, the door frames, all pure spirit. Men, animals and other beings—all pure spirit. Then, like a madman, I began to shower flowers in all directions. Whatever I saw, I worshipped."

Ramakrishna had adored the Mother with such ardor that he had come to see with her eyes, as her, and what he saw is what all the greatest mystics have seen: that daily life itself, in all of its activities, is a sacred dance of light. "Everything is holy!" Blake cried. A great Sufi mystic Dhu-L-Nun writes of an ecstasy he experienced: "I experienced this state from evening prayer until one third of the night was over, and I heard the voices of the creatures in the praise of God, with elevated voices so that I feared for my mind. I heard the fishes who said, 'Praised be the King, the most holy, the Lord.'" Are Dhu-L-Nun, Blake, Ramakrishna, Christ and the rest crazy, unhinged by adoration, or are we? Is Ramakrishna crazy to throw flowers in all directions, or are we crazy not to?

The road to adoration begins when we realize with a shock that what we call "normalcy" is in fact depression. Daily life is an uninterrupted dance of miracles, but only the eyes of love can see that.

The mystic traditions are essentially sciences of adoration, different ways suited to different temperaments to help the human being learn to adore and to play with his or her whole being variations on this great prayer composed by sweet Mother, Aurobindo's companion, to the Divine Mother:

> May all my speech and idle talk be mantra
> All actions of my hands be mudra (gestures of divine love and
>   knowledge)

> All eating and drinking be the offering of oblations unto thee
> All lying down be prostrations before thee
> May all pleasures be as dedicating my entire self unto thee
> May everything I do be taken as thy worship.

Enlightenment is the entire being praying that spontaneously at every moment.

MM: *For many of us, pride interferes with surrender and worship. Selfishness forces us to resist the extremest love that could lead us into communion.*

AH: I remember once in the early morning in Ladakh, listening to Bach's *Mass in B Minor*. I heard the words *Laudamus Te, Benedicimus Te, Adoramus Te, Glorificamus Te*, set to the sublime pulse of Bach's music and realized that the words of the Mass mirror the opening of the soul and what might be called the science of adoration.

Rilke says that "only in the hall of praise should lamentation go." The decision to praise, *Laudamus Te*, is the first and major decision of the spiritual life; knowing that it is through praise that the glory of the world will be revealed. This movement of celebration opens the heart on the journey towards God.

From this opening in praise comes a sense of reverence and joy, expressed in the words *Benedicimus Te*, we bless you. Praise initiates you into the glorious beauty of the Beloved and the intensity of the Beloved's tenderness towards each of us. At that moment, blessing arises in the human being; gratitude that the divine presence should be there, should be here, in such an abandon of splendor. Only then, when the heart is completely open, can we say *Adoramus Te*, we adore you. After praise and blessing, both of which are still partially distant relationships,

comes the inmost, intimate movement of adoration and so the
dawn of the possibility of fusion with the Source.

MM: *So there is another step beyond adoration?*

AH: Yes. The final relationship is represented by the final segment of
the Mass, *Glorificamus Te*. This is subtle; glorification is only
possible when you've tasted your own inner splendor through
adoration. The splendor of the Beloved and the splendor of the
love with which one loves the Beloved are revealed as the same
thing. "This" and "that" become a single energy. In glorifying with
our whole being, we ourselves become glorified. In opening in
adoration to the light, we call it down into us and unite with it
more and more.

One of Dante's supreme insights is that you rise in the universe
depending on your capacity for adoration. Adoration is the
energy of evolution. As a young man, Dante saw the young
Beatrice in a street. She shattered him with the radiance of
divine beauty reflecting through her; his life was troubled into
ecstasy and vision. Dante allowed that adoration to permeate
and possess him and to go on working on his inmost being for
years. Through this expansion of wonder at Beatrice, Dante
came to see that at every level of the universe, existence takes
its energy from creatures adoring the Divine. The snail and the
eagle adore God in their own ways, according to their dharma.
Even human sin and darkness conceal a hidden adoration.

The ascending rungs of paradise as described by Dante represent deepening levels of adoration until, as he says, saints like
Bonaventura and Francis become signs of fire. At the end of the
Paradiso, Dante is gazing into Beatrice's eyes and seeing the
universe. Adoration has so opened his heart that grace can

reflect the entire world there. Rumi echoes this gnosis by seeing
each stage of evolution as an ascension in adoration, an ascension that never ends. Adoration opens the heart to the infinity of
divine love, grows in passion to become more and more infinite
itself, so becoming the fuel of an ever-expanding growth, an
evolution in light without end. Rumi wrote:

> I died from minerality and became vegetable.
> And from vegetativeness I died and became animal.
> I died from animality and became man.
> Then why fear disappearance through death?
> Next time I shall die bringing forth wings and feathers like angels;
> After that, soaring higher than angels—what you cannot imagine,
> I shall be that.

MM: *You can think of adoration as the fuel of evolution. You can also know it as a way of remembering origin.*

AH: Yes, adoration heals the wound of separation from origin. Human experience is a crawling back through spirals of worship to the light that gave birth to you in the first place. The energy that takes you back through these spirals is adoration. And it is the same energy that takes you forward and upward; as Heraclitus said: "The way up is the way down," and vice versa.

MM: *It's like the planets circling the sun, with everything adhering to light. Meher Baba described gravity as an act of love on the cosmic scale. Still, in our everyday living with its egotism and limitations, it's often hard just getting along with other people, let alone adoring them.*

AH: Each of us has to begin where we are, using what we have. Think of Christopher Smart's poem "My Cat Geoffrey," in which he enumerates all the perfections of his strange tabby! If you love flowers, look at the chrysanthemum or the camellia as a sign of divine beauty. If you love men or women, practice seeing their beauty as Whitman does, as "letters from God dropped in the street." Start with your desires and simple loves, and follow that love higher and higher to its origin, the house of love itself. All the different human loves are like fragrances that the Beloved leaves behind in the room. You can follow those fragrances until you arrive in the room where the Beloved is. You realize then that every form of love is a reflection of this one experience.

MM: *With grief being a darker reflection.*

AH: Yes, as we've said, the yoga of adoration—and indeed all of spiritual life—begins when we stop protecting ourselves from feeling. With that opening of the heart, the pain of the world becomes a great sense of intimate communion. An acute sense of mortality, combined with the poignancy of time passing, breeds a love for all things. When my grandmother was dying of cancer, she wanted to live to see the roses in her garden in June. When they came, it was as if she was seeing the fullness and glory of the world for the first time: Christ's blood flowing through the rose. She was a devout Christian living this experience as the Resurrection.

That love is open to us all, but its deepest consummation is the love of the master, because he or she is the only thing worthy of perfect love, the one to whom we can give completely without fear. Until you meet that being, there will always be something incomplete in the progress toward adoration. Every other human love always contains a grain of desolation—what the Buddha called "duhkha"—something that can't be worked through. Although this is part of the beauty and challenge of loving imperfect beings, the relationship with the master offers the opportunity for a boundless and perfect love, a vessel into which you can pour your complete inner madness.

MM: *Why do you call it madness?*

AH: At it's greatest, it is a mad relationship in the Sufi sense. The master is saying, "Love me completely, give me everything, and I will change it into gold."

MM: *That reminds me of the story of God coming disguised to two men and asking them both for all their money. One gives him a coin or two, and that is turned to gold. The other gives him everything in his pockets, and everything he has is transformed. God can only give you back what you are willing to give to God.*

AH: In the relationship with a perfect master, you realize that you can trust him or her with your very life. That breeds a capacity for adoration which is unlike anything else in human existence.

MM: *The trouble with madness is that it implies insanity.*

AH: The process can involve what psychology might call a psychotic break. Meditation slowly peels away and exposes the fact that all the constructions that the ego makes of reality are absolutely plausible and absolutely false. It is then that the full wildness of Divine Reality—the force which is creating a thousand disasters and a thousand births, supernovas, nightmare and revelation as we speak—starts to dawn in the open consciousness.

Ordinary consciousness reels before what it is discovering. There is terror in the reeling, because the naked Divine Reality is without boundaries, ordinary morality or anything which we can control in any way. The soul is then invited to enter into the

Divine's ecstatic dance of life and death, to know what Rumi means when he says, "One day at your wine shop, I drank a little wine and threw off the robe of this body. Drunk on you, this world is harmony. Creation, destruction, I'm dancing for them both."

To unite the paradoxes, to dance as the sacred androgyne, is to be completely out of your mind in the eyes of reason. The destruction of boundaries and categories puts you into the wordless place where nothing survives but God, where all multiplicity is seen as dancing sparks of the secret fire. That madness is the essential being of each of us, and it is what the mystic risks incarnating through adoration. Rumi says, "If you find me, hide me in your heart, know my madness as absolute truth."

MM: *We're in paradox again—sanity is madness, and madness, the deepest sanity.*

AH: St. Paul says that the wisdom of men is the madness of fools. At the end of "In Praise of Folly," after looking at all the different ways in which the world is crazy—for sex, money, power—Erasmus agrees that the true folly is the folly of the saints. This is the folly that heals divisions and illuminates, drops like a bomb on the prison of reason and allows you to parachute out. By opening to everything, even horror can be transmuted into ecstasy.

I was once in the shore temple in Mahabalipuram, an ancient place sacred to Shiva in south India. There was an old beggar woman in rags worshipping the lingam there. Suddenly, a storm broke out and ocean waves began to crash over her. The wilder the sea became, the crazier the wind, the louder she sang and the more passionately she danced, drenched as she was and in danger of being washed out to sea. I saw by the burning in her eyes that she had understood the secret.

MM: *Haven't you found that what looks like danger and loss can actually be a secret door to opening and adoration?*

AH: There's a beautiful essay by Adrian Stokes in which he describes leaving a garden that he'd been wrestling with for years, in which brambles grew like grass, in which every rose seemed to wither immediately. As he was leaving, he turned and looked at the garden and realized that underneath all the superficial disorder, the garden had always been perfect. His heart flooded with joy and relief. "The Mother was always present in the garden," he wrote. Why was he always trying to twist it into another shape? Why hadn't he simply adored it?

MM: *Isn't that the story of our lives? Rumi says that "the bird of paradise is born from the ashes of illusion." Ashes and sweetness become variations on the same wisdom. You mentioned the Mother just now. How does the yoga of adoration tie specifically into the path of the Divine Feminine?*

AH: Adoration is the gift, the power, the devotional form of the path of the sacred feminine, the direct way into the Mother's heart of light.

The Divine Mother is, I believe, saying three things to the world today. First, we are being asked to adore her in all her aspects, terrible and sublime, and by so doing, offer her whatever we can for her great sacrifice.

MM: *Anandamayi Ma has said that her food is "dedicated lives." And the second thing she is asking us?*

AH: "Adore each being as my child." In this, we are encouraged to bring to our relationships with all sentient beings—animals, plants and insects as well as humans—a tiny spark of the

Mother's infinite tenderness. In one of his letters, Coleridge says that the great poet exhibits "the tenderness of a blind man stroking the face of his only daughter." This is the tenderness of the Mother. This is the tenderness that the Mother is asking us to show to everything now, to each other and everything in the creation. How could we harm other people if we saw who they actually were, divine children infinitely precious to the Mother? How could we go on devastating nature if we knew it as her and our body? The cruelty and madness around us would come to an end. And we could find in us also that power of forgiveness that heals the past and births the future.

MM: *The tenderness of the Mother opens us to the pain of the torturer as well as the victim.*

AH: Yes. Adoration teaches us to reach into the core of the torturer's suffering and to pray for their release from the prison of desolation which is causing them to act with cruelty. In the memoir *Dialogue with an Angel*, an angel takes control of a Hungarian girl, Lily, who died in a concentration camp and delivers, through her, an extraordinary message to the world. Survivors have described how Lily died: singing in hell, having helped hundreds of people, her heart completely open. How can we know what power the angel's adoration bestowed on Lily in those final moments, the power not only to irradiate the souls of those being murdered with her, but of those murdering as well? Living the angel's message in hell, she became the angel. This is what the Mother is asking us to do in our own extreme situation.

MM: *And the Mother's third message to us?*

AH: "Adore yourself as my beloved child, light of my light." This is perhaps the hardest message of all to enact, and the secret condition for all the others. What does adoring yourself in this highest sense mean? It means being grateful for the whole of existence, for the miracle of being in a body in her womb of light, the universe, to be grateful for having ears so precise that they can hear the forty parts of the Tallis motet! Grateful for having eyes so clear that you can perceive the tiny beads of frost on the rose, each one glittering with the dawn sunlight. Grateful for the feast of joy and pain being spread for us here. Through this adoration of yourself as the Mother's child, life becomes a conscious dance of wondering connection with her and in her. You come to see her face of love turned toward you at all times and in all events.

MM: *How can people—particularly those who do not believe in God—begin to feel this gratitude?*

AH: Everyone must begin from where he or she is. I've seen many atheists fall silent in the presence of the Dalai Lama. Some of the fragrance of his enlightenment is blown toward them. In parables in the New Testament, you find people giving up their fear in Christ's presence simply because he was so full of love. As always, hope lies in the truth that we all have the Buddha Nature working in us to bring us to the recognition of our divinity, regardless of how long it takes. That is why the mystics never give up. They know that the secret order of the universe is on their side. However appalling the suffering of the world is, its ultimate nature is *sat-chit-ananda*, love-knowledge-joy.

MM: *And adoration is especially crucial because it reconnects us with reverence for the creation and for preserving it.*

AH: The Mother has an essential role at this moment because we are in danger of losing those visionary and nourishing capacities which are distinctly feminine and connected to the genius of the natural world. I believe it is in the Aborigines that we see the understanding of this genius at its purest. For them, everything in the natural world is a symbolic footprint of the metaphysical beings whose actions created it. The power of every earthly place for them is thus wedded to the memory of its origin, and this power the Aborigines called the dreaming of a place. This dreaming constitutes the sacredness of the earth they sustain by singing their way into the world, by wrapping the whole world in a web of song. These "songlines" are their own veins and arteries, so they in their singing and their world with its rocks and rivers, and the power that is manifesting all of this is known to be one. Adoration for them breeds total respect and total recognition, for the earth they know is a symbolic language, a memory of origin, everywhere instilled with a sacred order that must not be disturbed.

MM: *This emphasis on adoration and embrace of the creation differs totally, as we've said, from the patriarchal ideal of transcendence.*

AH: Unfortunately, as I said when we spoke of the sacred feminine, so many of the patriarchal mystics have stressed detachment from the world and escape into the Absolute. In this way, certain types of mysticism have actually conspired unconsciously with the destruction of the world by stressing a flight from matter and a condemnation of nature as fallen and dead.

While strong on transcendence, as you've said, these patriarchal mystics have not honored what Hildegard of Bingen called *viriditas*, the greenness of things, the shooting energy which is the *shakti* manifesting everything. With the threatening of the earth in this dark age, escapism and condemnation of matter and nature are no longer options. Only the Mother who is all love, tenderness and embrace can work with the terrible self-disgust that humankind feels at having done so much harm to itself and to nature. Only adoring her, and the sacred feminine that is her, can give us the insight and vision we now need. Nothing is disgusting to her, and to her nothing is impossible. However deeply we betray and mutilate ourselves or the planet, she will never abandon us, her children. Even if we were to destroy the part of creation she has given us to guard, she still would never hate or abandon us. Her love is infinite, beyond all conditions, eternal. If we let our hearts open in wonder and adoration to that love now, before it is too late, and to the light that is streaming from that love toward us to heal us, anything, anything at all, is possible.

19

THE DIVINE CHILD

O holy yoga of adoration, melting all fears
All places the false self could hide to save itself
To find the heart of the child behind the door of scars
That golden room where all things blaze.

—For the Mother
Andrew Harvey

In manifesting the world, Tao becomes the universal Mother.
In the knowledge of the Mother is the knowledge of her children.
And this childhood being known, there is access to the Mother.

—Tao-Te-Ching

MM: *Of all the images of spiritual mastery—the hermit, the yogi, the magus, the*
martyr, the priest-king—that of the child has always seemed to me at once
the most magical, the most mysterious and the most difficult for someone
brought up in a power-and-control obsessed society like ours to grasp. And
yet, the image of the child is central to all mystic traditions. Teresa of Avila
was asked on her deathbed what, after her death, she would teach all the souls
who turned to her. She said she would urge them to embark on the way of
spiritual childhood, the path of confidence and complete abandon.

AH: This is the key of keys, the secret of secrets. After enlightenment,
the Buddha entered child-mind, the kingdom of primal wonder

and innocence. Heraclitus, greatest of the early Greek mystics, wrote, "The kingdom is the child's." Ramana Maharshi and Ramakrishna again and again tell us that the nature of God is childlike, and that the realized being is like a child at peace in the womb of the mother, knowing he or she is fed at every moment by the grace and the light of the Mother. The Christian alchemists tell us that when in our being we have completed the sacred marriage of opposites, of the male and the female, the sun and the moon, the dark and the light, the conscious and the unconscious, we become a sacred androgyne-child, free of reason's madness and the ego's frivolous gloom, free of all conscious and unconscious barriers and definitions, mysterious and complete as reality itself and one with its mystery in the ground of our perfected being.

MM: *Didn't Christ say, "Unless you become again as little children you cannot enter again the kingdom of heaven"?*

AH: The "as" in that sentence is revelatory. None of the supreme mystics are talking about a regression into fantasy, an abandonment of discrimination, proper self-protection and the hard-earned insights of adult suffering, work and sacrifice necessary for survival in the world. What they are pointing to is a state of conscious, lucid childlikeness that is the most luminous possible opposite of regression, and that contains, while completing and transcending, all other forms of knowledge and wisdom. As Blake said, "Unorganized innocence is an impossibility." This state of consciously, athletically reclaimed childhood, in which all the passion, pure sensuality and lyricism of the lost or hidden child is consciously reintegrated into a purified and "organized" adult awareness is the end of yoga and the attainment of the kingdom of heaven itself. To be a child in this glorious sense is to be in heaven here, to be one with the Tao, to possess the Grail, to be in union with the Mother.

Lewis Thompson wrote, "The ever-new magical universe is continually reborn in the child. Only the grownup was banished from Eden. The child eats of the tree of life. For him the laws of the universe are magical. This childhood and this magic the Christ restores." In a supremely beautiful passage in the ninth chapter of his *De Calculo*, Ruysbroeck writes, making a crucial difference between the secret friend, the yogi, the adept and the hidden child of God: "How great is the difference...for the friend makes only loving, living but reasoned ascents towards God. But the child presses on to lose his own life upon the summits, in that simplicity which does not know itself...When we transcend ourselves and become in our ascent towards God so simple that the bare supreme love can lay hold on us, then we cease, and we and all our selfhood die in God. And in this death we become the hidden children of God, and find a new life within us."

MM: *The whole meaning of the spiritual search is to birth this child in us.*

AH: And when it is born, it lives in the fullness of God, in which there is, as Ruysbroeck again says, "tranquility according to his essence, activity according to his nature; absolute repose, absolute fecundity." Only the divine child can be at once reposeful and fecund, because the child unites Siva and Shakti, the male and the female, the silence and the force, in its own intimate being and is then released to dance for God in God as a part of God. To be like this is at once to enter, to be and to recreate in and around you, paradise. Around those who have become like children, miracles dance. As divine children, we can do anything, or rather, anything can be done by God through us.

And in place of the limited, precarious protection that the ego gives us, we will be protected by the Divine itself.

MM: *You're saying that the transformation the human race must make can only be done as "hidden children"?*

AH: Yes. Think of Ramakrishna. He is the greatest, sweetest, most sublime child of the Divine Mother, and the clue to the transformation in her. Has anyone been more gloriously the hidden child than him? Again and again, almost obsessively, in the Gospel of Ramakrishna, the saint returns to the theme of the child, knowing that the whole secret is there. "When the dry branch of a coconut palm drops to the ground, it leaves only a mark on the trunk indicating that once there was a branch at that place. In like manner, he who has attained God keeps only an appearance of ego…and he becomes like a child." And he goes on to say that a "child has no attachment. He becomes as quickly detached from a thing as he becomes attached to it. He has no feeling of high and low in regard to persons…the child doesn't know hate or what is holy or unholy." Elsewhere he says that the child is closest to God because God has the nature of a child. God himself, in the mystery of his *lila*, or divine play, is childlike.

Ramakrishna pictures God as a child sitting by the side of the road with gems in the skirt of his cloth. "Many a person passes him by along the road. Many…pray to him for gems. But he hides the gems with his hands and says, turning away his face, 'No, I will not give any away.' But another man comes along. He doesn't ask for the gems, and yet the child runs after him and offers him the gems, begging him to accept them." Reality itself, the Mother herself, is a child, sweet, wild, pure, unpredictable as a child and only the child has the trust, the openness, the fabulous flexibility always to be attuned to and at one with it, and with her.

Ramakrishna used to pray again and again to have all powers, occult and otherwise, taken from him, to be and know and live in only pure love for the Mother. And yet, who could have been more "powerful" than he?

For many years, I did not really understand this paradox, but recently it became clear. When Ramakrishna gave up all his own power for love of the Mother, the power of the Mother could flow unbrokenly and ecstatically in continual play through him and so change history. As her child, her power was his: Ramakrishna was free to be transparent to her and transmit her and radiate her at every moment and with every breath and so create around him and for all those who love him, even now, her playground of miracle. It is through each of us taking up Ramakrishna's challenge to be totally, ecstatically and in childlike wonder transparent to her that the Mother will be able to work through us the wonder she is preparing for the world. The lamp of power will only be given to Aladdin, for only Aladdin's heart is innocent and loving, and his will desires only the feast of God. The future will be made by her and for her by humble, illumined, playful, divine children.

MM: *And like Ramakrishna, the hidden children of the Mother will wear a smile.*

AH: Yes. The secret smile on the face of the Cycladic Mothers, on the Kores of archaic Greece, on the face of the Buddha, on the face of the dolphin. The smile that is the ultimate sign of realization, the smile of deathlessness, fearlessness and welcome.

Part Four

20

DARKNESS

The keys of the Unknowable are gathered all on his level: He alone knows them.

—The Koran

> *Deep in the wine vault of*
> *my love I drank, and when I came*
> *out on this open meadow*
> *I knew nothing at all.*

—St. John of the Cross

MM: *Let's talk now about the destination of all these many steps along the path. In all the mystical traditions it is agreed that divine knowledge can only come when all concepts are abandoned, when we enter the darkness and rest there to learn its secrets.*

AH: Yes. The highest state as the greatest mystics of all the traditions have told us—from Eckhart and St. Dionysius in the West to Shankara and Ibn Arabi and Nagarjuna in the East—is not divine knowledge, but divine "ignorance." All knowledge, however exact, contracts, maintains a difference, however transparent, between knower and known, seer and seen. The ultimate state will not split into seer and seen. You can *be* that ultimate state, but you can never *know* it as an object, either of

worship or science or vision. Lao Tzu wrote, "The man of learning gains every day. The man of Tao loses every day." Every day
the mystic loses—loses knowing, loses dualistic hopes and
visions, loses, as Ken Wilber says, "any form of grasping or
seeking, and rests instead in divine ignorance, in the cloud of
unknowing, which for Lao Tzu was the great mystery, the mystery
of pure awareness which can never be known or grasped and yet
contains the entire majesty before your eyes right at this
moment." The heart and mind have to enter in profoundest love
into the night of God, what Tauler calls "deep yet dazzling
darkness…dark from its surpassing brightness…as the shining
of the sun on its course is as darkness to weak eyes."

The great Christian mystic Gregory of Nysssa tells us that there
are three stages of ascent toward God. The first he calls the
purgative way, which is the purification that frees the seeker
from the past and from grief. The second is the illuminative way,
that of opening to the divine mystery, seeing the divine light in
all things. Third is the way of darkness, in which the darkness
beyond the light is entered, and in that darkness the final love
beyond concept or dogma or reason is experienced—what Bede
Griffiths beautifully calls "the unity of love in the dark." This is
the experience of love beyond knowledge, experienced in
darkness, and it is in this love that Isaiah's promise is fulfilled: "I
will give you the treasures of darkness and the hidden riches of
secret places."

MM: *And it is in this darkness that the heights of the mystical life are scaled.*

AH: A great Sufi master Dhu-L-Nun remarked: "Whatever you
imagine, God is the opposite of that." Dionysius says, "The
Godhead surpasses all condition, movement, life, imagination,
conjecture, name, discourse, thought, conception, being, rest,

dwelling, limit, infinity, everything that exists." All language, all knowing of any kind must be defective, and all definitions of the Absolute are prisons, reflections of the observer's need and limitation and not of the reality.

To come to know God, we must go beyond all these names and forms and concepts, and go into the Divine darkness. For all the great mystics, the soul's task is to lose herself in that which can be neither seen nor touched, to become united to the unknown by the most noble part of herself. To embrace what can never be understood is the source of all transformative understanding and to go again and again with willing and humble trust into the night of God is to experience the mystery of Absolute love and the unity of all opposites, a unity incomprehensible to the mind unless it is illumined by a "ray of the divine darkness."

MM: *The Sufi mystic Shabestari tells us that when a visible thing is entirely close to us, the corporeal eye cannot see it.*

AH: It's just the same with the interior eye. When the seeker on the way of God, in order to arrive at the Deity, transcends the light of the manifestations of the names and attributes, he or she becomes capable of receiving the epiphany of the divine essence.

MM: *The light of this epiphany seems to the seeker like a black light because of its proximity and intensity.*

AH: Exactly. The eye of the seeker darkens and cannot perceive it. In that dazzled blindness, we humans at last can enter the glory of God. As Dionysius says, "When love has carried us above and beyond all things, above the light, into the divine dark, there we are worked on the transformed by the eternal Word who is the image of the Father." Mystics throughout the ages have tried and failed to describe this state. When Rumi speaks of the night where "He and I are lost in love," and when Novalis speaks of the "great fecundity of darkness" in his splendid hymns to the night, they are both celebrating the power of this highest nocturnal mystery to engender and to go on and on engendering new being, new gnosis.

MM: *Is this state related to the black Madonna?*

AH: Yes. There is a whole tradition of mystic understanding that begins from the phrase in the Bible, "She is black but beautiful." This tradition came to be known as the cult of Sophia. Wisdom was thought of as black, arising as it does from the willingness to enter into the darkness of divine mystery. Blackness is central to the miraculous process of growth. You put a seed into the darkness of the winter ground, and it comes up in spring. This process is parallel to what happens in the psyche. In grief, all sorts of secret processes are taking place in the dark which will lead to opportunities for growth. "In a dark time, the eye begins to see," wrote Theodore Roethke. Darkness trains the eye; it forces you to look at dark things and gives you a preternatural sensitivity. That's why cats had a holy significance for the Egyptians; they had the gift of seeing in the dark. The black Madonna has the capacity to see in the night, then to gestate and be fecund. The womb of the Divine Mother, the mysterious darkness of the Tao, gives birth to divine light. The black Madonna is the dark matrix of this endless divine birth. The way of the feminine invites us to enter that darkness, to break gently apart in that womb, to be remade as a divine child who is happy to re-enter the dark again and again, aware that this darkness is the source itself of light, this "divine ignorance" a constant fountain of gnosis.

MM: *In Hinduism, the sacredness of the dark mother emanates from Kali, the*
black one. She is the ferocious, mysterious mother whose body combines
destruction and creation. Ramakrishna sings to her in his Gospel:

> *In dense darkness, O Mother, thy formless*
> *beauty sparkles;*
> *Therefore the yogis meditate in a dark mountain cave.*
> *In the lap of boundless dark, on Mahanirvana's*
> *waves upborne, Peace flows serene*
> *and inexhaustible.*
> *Taking the form of the Void, in the robe*
> *of darkness wrapped,*
> *Why art thou, Mother, seated alone*
> *in the shrine of samadhi?*
> *From the Lotus of Thy fear-scattering*
> *feet flash Thy love's lightnings;*
> *Thy Spirit-face shines forth with*
> *laughter terrible and loud!*

AH: We also find this reverence for the mystery of darkness, "this
dark formless beauty," in Islam. At the center of the Muslim
world is the *kaaba*, the stone building in the court of the great
mosque at Mecca which contains a sacred black stone, around
which hundreds of thousands of pilgrims turn, imitating the
turning of the worlds and stars in their heavenly dance around
an unknowable mystery.

MM: *And the ego's passion for security and hunger for conclusions are exactly*
what the mystic must give up.

AH: The mystic realizes that only by making of him- or herself a dark,
patient womb can the light come in. Only by entering the cloud
of unknowing can the true knowledge go on being given. So the

mystic life is a commitment to a special form of open ignorance. Rilke said angels come only to beginners; the mystic remains a beginner in every second, like the cosmos itself which goes on being perpetually reborn.

MM: *It's no wonder that mystic experience cannot be confirmed in any rational way.*

AH: How could it be? It requires a surrender of all limited "knowing," a continual reimmersion in the innocence of darkness, a happy blindness the rational mind reels at. Remember that Saul had to pass through a period of blindness, when Christ appeared to him, before he could become Paul. He needed to undergo total stripping in order to attain a new name. At the height of his wisdom, Oedipus at Colonus has two dark eyes which have been obliterated by tragedy and the light of divine awareness. Tiresias has two dark eyes as well, having seen the fire of the Divine flaming up at him. The pupils of their worldly reason have been pierced. The ancient association of blindness with wisdom pays tribute to the way in which the eyes of the ego have to be put out in order for gnosis to be born and installed in the core of the being.

MM: *Let's go back to the mystic path. I'm fascinated by the way blindness, darkness and death weave together in this process of denuding and enlightenment.*

AH: The connection is vital. In the Sufi system of lights, the black light is considered one of the holiest of all. It is only revealed to the most accomplished masters, those who have vanished themselves in the process known as *fana*, annihilation of the ego. For millennia, shamans of every indigenous culture have described the horror of this process, one which is incomprehensible to those who have not been through it. This mystic death is nothing less than being torn apart in the night by God. There is ecstasy in being torn apart by God, but also pain that must be consented to. The agony of dismemberment, the darkness of Gethsemene, has to be accepted. As one Persian mystic said, "Without the Friday of the Crucifixion, there would be no Sunday of the Resurrection." Those are the terms. The mystic has to pass through the halls of death while in a body. Meister Eckhart said that "If you do not die before you die, you die when you die." Bursevi, the Sufi mystic, wrote of this state: "This death must come about by resolution and he in whom this state of death appears will see the complete annihilation of everything but God. . .Nothing is left but the beauty of God."

MM: *And in this movement toward the light through darkness, you must accept every form of evil as part of the One, not separate from it.*

AH: To run into the light, as so many of us are tempted to do, is revealed eventually as another form of evasion and cowardice. What's needed, as we've said, is a *coincidentia oppositorum*, a sacred marriage of opposites, both light and dark, to reach the point at which darkness and light fuse in a nuclear explosion of insight and absolute unconditional love. The mystic comes to live at that nuclear point. At this point what is known and lived is, as Bursevi tells us, that "the reality, in its qualities, in its descent and its degrees accepts the opposites because from its point of view there is no such thing as opposite. . .there is not a single relative in which there is not a face of the Absolute. . .what is seen in the mirrors of the two universes is one face."

MM: *In fact, the experience of evil becomes part of the complete initiation into nonduality or unity consciousness.*

AH: When I first went back to India at twenty-five, I visited a certain

holy place in northern India and had two of the most frightening
and revealing experiences of my life on the same morning. There
is a temple where thousands of rats are worshipped and fed. I
have a peculiar horror of rats, but I forced myself to go into this
place. You stand on a platform and peer into the darkness.
Soon, you see that the darkness is actually swarming.

Spiritually, I felt challenged in a way I'd never known before. I
realized that until I could bless this swarming darkness, I knew
nothing. I could talk about loving creation, but until I could love
this horror, I had no right to make that claim. What's more, I had
to accept that I was that darkness. Until I could look at the part of
my "being" that was just a swarming night of rats, an absolute
abomination, I would never understand myself. It was that part of
my being that had created concentration camps and was destroying the environment. Until I acknowledged it as mine, until I
found the holiness in this black part, I could not transform it.

I reeled out of the temple and turned down an alleyway where I
saw a completely naked man sitting in a pile of cow dung, eating
it with the most ecstatic expression on his face, like a baby
eating chocolate. He belonged to the caste known as *aghoris*,
considered to be among the holiest men in India, those who
have shattered all boundaries, dissolved all shame, transcended
all norms. I was repulsed, terrified to the core of my being but
knew I was before a sacred mystery.

MM: *What happens in that mystery?*

AH: If you can endure it and allow it to unfold within you, the
androgyne is born inside you through shamelessness, through
total abandoned acceptance. In the mysterious process of
blessing everything that we have hitherto considered disgusting

and obscene in ourselves and in reality, we discover the extraordinary power, the alchemical *Kali* power that's hidden in that obscenity. When you can truly bless excrement, truly bless sexuality, violence, death, dismemberment in all their aspects without fear or rage or bitterness or any trace of reservation, then you have broken forever the barriers that chain you to duality. You have transcended fear of any possible kind and all egocentric forms of grief. It's a very dangerous path; you can easily become intoxicated with the power that is revealed to you or go mad or be torn apart by the forces you are confronting. You should only do it, if at all, with the help of a master, and in a state of complete devotion to the master. But whatever path you take, there is no doubt that without blessing the dark, the disquieting, the uncanny and terrible, you cannot ascend or come to the place at which you are one with reality. Every aspect of Kali has to be adored: the mother that births and the mother that devours and devastates and destroys. When you can adore both the terrifying and the golden face of Kali, know them as two faces of one life and praise them both in total acceptance with the full passion of a being at peace with everything, then you are free from duality forever. Like the *aghori*, you are naked, holding onto nothing, no "belief" no "concept" no "definition" of any kind, led from moment to moment by the hand of the Mother, reality itself. You know that you are both at one with and free from whatever appears, both dead and alive in a life beyond "life" or "death." As Meister Eckhart says: "By aligning itself with God's will, the soul takes on the taste of God: grief and joy, bitterness and sweetness, darkness and light, all become divine."

MM: *You are saying that behind our aversions and self-disgust are reservoirs of love and sanctity, reservoirs, in fact, of the highest wisdom waiting to be revealed and made available.*

AH: Yes. By witnessing the *aghori's* unconditional abandon to all things, I learned that what this naked man was doing literally, we must all do. We must learn fearlessly to eat our death, our heartbreak and the agony of the world, in order to learn how to taste the bliss in even the most appalling suffering and distress, a bliss that transcends totally all categories of the mind. Ramakrishna dying blessed even the pain of his throat cancer, blessed the presence of the Mother even in the core of that agony. I had the grace to be with Bede Griffiths when he was dying. He was in infinite pain but knew Christ and the Mother were also in that pain, and that knowledge kept on opening and opening him to more and more astonishing outpourings of blessing and love. By accepting completely the horror of the dying that was devastating him, he could turn each moment of agony, of loss, of humiliation into a more and more profound, more and more heart- and soul-piercing gesture of tenderness, or courage, or gratitude and so initiate all those who were blessed to be with him into the reality of Christ and the Mother and the reality of the presence of resurrection even in the heart of the darkness of crucifixion.

I was once in a train with a man who had been among the first to enter Dachau after the war. He described what it was like to go into the gates of this seemingly deserted place and then to see the people, or what had been people, coming dazedly from those huts. The only thing he could do was to fall to his knees. There's a way in which, when you finally face terminal horror, the only response is to fall onto your knees, to beg in every cell of your body for light and healing. This man told me that it was the first time that he had ever felt the presence of God, seeing what the ego stripped of divinity could do. So the Divine, even in that absence, even in that final, abominable absence, was present.

MM: *Still we wonder what kind of God would allow Dachau.*

AH: This is a mystery that terrifies and transcends reason. The
       darkness of God contains Auschwitz, spinabifida and all the
       appalling suffering of the innocents we see around us. This
       paradox of evil within absolute good cannot be understood by
       the mind, but it can be lived and loved in the heart. Let us look
       at Job. God gave Satan permission to afflict Job in unspeakable
       ways, testing him right to the end. Job remained at the center of
       darkness without complaining, always praising. As De Caussade
       wrote so movingly of him, "His ruin he regarded as one of God's
       names, and in blessing it, he was declaring that, no matter how
       terrible its manifestations, it was always holy, under whatever
       name or form it appeared."

       At the end of the story, Job isn't told anything; he is given a
       direct vision of the Absolute, a vision that in some mysterious
       sense affliction prepared him for. Like Arjuna in the Gita, Job
       sees the entire cosmos irradiated by the fire of God's bound-
       less and infinite glory. What cures him is not an answer but a
       transcendental ecstasy. He becomes one with the one beyond
       all questions, all knowledge, sees the absolute splendor of
       God, bows down to it in a total adoration that brings him, I
       believe, enlightenment. Infinite pain and infinite love take him
       to the point at which he can disappear into the dark silence of
       God and be reborn in the eternal light. No one has expressed
       this highest of all states more marvelously than Ruysbroeck:
       "In this return in love in the divine ground every divine way and
       activity and all the attributes of the persons are swallowed up
       in the rich compass of the essential unity. All the divine means
       and all conditions, and all living images which are reflected in
       the mirror of truth, lapse in the onefold and ineffable wayless-
       ness, beyond reason. Here there is nothing but eternal rest in

the fruitive embrace of an outpouring love. This is the dark silence in which all lovers lose themselves."

21

SILENCE

How long does the bee buzz about? As long as it is not sitting on a flower. No sooner does it rest on a flower than it keeps quiet.

—Ramakrishna

In silent wonder the wise see him as the life flaming in all creation.

—Mundaka Upanishad

> *He came all so still*
> *Where his Mother was*
> *As dew in April*
> *That falls on the grass.*

—Medieval carol for the Virgin

MM: *In the end, of course, is silence, and the merging of self with Unity. You mentioned nonduality just now—what the Hindus call* advaita. *This is a tough concept for Judeo-Christian materialists to absorb.*

AH: *Advaita* is not monism. *Advaita* means "not-two." We and the universe are not "one": then all distinctions would be destroyed. We are "not-two," intricately interrelated with everything, both separate, unique, *and* united. The astonishment of this dance of "not-two" grows slowly as the mind and heart open in divine love and wisdom. Imagine that there was a heap of gold and a skillful smith. The smith made fir trees, geraniums, tables, human beings, lamps. Every object had a different shape, a different purpose and identity but was made of the same thing. Look at the sea. All waves are rising and falling differently, in different rhythms, with different volumes. Some catch the light, some do not. You can see the separations between the waves, but what you also see quite clearly is that all the waves are water. That is what the knowledge of "not-two" is like. Things retain the separateness which the senses give them, which we use to negotiate this reality, but the illumined mind knows that all things are Brahman, waves of one infinite sea of light. You know, in other words, that you and everything and the light that is at all times manifesting everything are "not-two," and "you" come to exist normally on all levels of the divine creation, and meet "yourself" in all states, events, conditions, beings. This is *sahaja*, spontaneous negotiation of and union with all dimensions at all moments. Nisargadatta Maharaj explains most lucidly the marvelous transitions to this state: "When the I am myself goes, the I am all comes. When the I am all goes, the I am comes. When even I am goes, Reality alone is and in it every I am is preserved and glorified."

It is wonderful that this the most ultimate and holy of all possible experiences in this world, that of unity, of *advaita*, has to be enjoyed by everyone in their own profound solitude, at that diamond point of solitude at which everyone secretly joins and meets God and each other and all things. This final experience is kept for this most sacred and secret moment and is too vast and precious to be ever completely communicated. This is the moment when the created one returns to the source of creation, the moment at which all laws, dogmas and techniques that

helped the mystic arrive at that diamond point vanish in the
silence of return to origin.

MM: *Not only at the end of the path, but all along it, the Divine comes softly into
the being and must be listened for with great quietness As Meher Baba, who
was silent for the last forty-four years of his life said, "Things that are Real
are given and received in silence."*

AH: Yes, silence is both the starting point, the ground and the goal,
as masters of every sacred technology have indicated. In fact,
mysticism may be said to be the science of silence. Mystics leap
constantly into silence in order to rest there and to allow its
secret laws and energies to operate upon their being. If that leap
is complete, the revelations needed for enlightenment can be
given. Silence can then open the soul to the full music of all its
different dimensions. As Angelus Silesius says, "The angels sing
beautifully, I know though that if you are only silence, your
singing delights more the supreme."

MM: *And how are silence and enlightenment so profoundly linked?*

AH: Silence, in its essence, is Presence, active, brimming, electric
Presence. All mystical experience, from the first glimmers of
insight to the dawning of divine light, take place in that rapt
dazzling silence of God, that silence which Ramana Maharshi
said, is "unceasing eloquence."

MM: *And isn't this silence what we hear behind the words of the greatest
scriptures?*

AH: Yes. Sacred languages are vibrant with its holy energy. In
Sanskrit, for instance, sound is considered to be the distilled
power of silence. To listen to the Vedas being chanted is to be

initiated, through stillness of mind, into the Word, the logos, out of which all things arise. Poets such as the ones who created these scriptures live their lives at the level of serene intensity which silence engenders. From their attention to holy silence arise the words that they use; words designed to draw the mind deep into the heart, in whose silent light it can be baptized again and again and again expanded, illumined and transformed. In essence, sacred poetry is the inexpressible being heard, the moon of language radiant with the sun of silence. When this divine silence is present, words have direct initiatory power, are themselves flames of the fire of silence.

MM: *As a culture, we've forgotten how to be quiet and receptive. Silence begins where theologies end.*

AH: Ramana Maharshi sent a note to Paul Brunton just before he left the body, saying, "When heart speaks to heart, what more is there to say?" When the enlightened heart of the master and the awakening heart of the disciple are in a state of union, no words are necessary. Reality becomes the golden book in which the love poem of relationship is constantly being renewed and written and rewritten.

MM: *There is a certain moment when verbal teaching is no longer necessary.*

AH: Words serve a certain, limited purpose, satisfying the mind. But, as Ramakrishna pointed out, the mind will take you to the courtyard of the Beloved, but only the heart will lead you to His or Her bedroom, where, as the Gita says, "When the heart has found quietness, wisdom has also found peace."

MM: *The most sacred experience is surrounded by fires of secrecy, silence, unknowing.*

AH: And when the initiate finally returns to the normal world to give some account of what has been seen, the best he or she can do through mere words is lead the mind to the point where it is brave enough to let the enormity of God silence it. As Amiel writes in his journal, "Our languages have no words to express…this heavenly quietness, this ocean of peace which both reflects the heavens above and is master of its own vast depth."

How marvelous this is, for it means that nothing can ever sully the ultimate experience. As Ramakrishna says, "All things in the world—the Vedas, the Puranas, the Tantras, the six systems of philosophy—have been defiled, like food that has been touched by the tongue. Only one thing has not been defiled in this way and that is Brahman. No one has ever been able to say what Brahman is." And no one has been or will ever be able to say what the Mother is, who is one with Brahman. Al-Hallat, the supreme Sufi mystic says of this silence: "The third and highest degree of *tawhid* (the unity of God) is the one that God has chosen for Himself, the one of which He alone is worthy; and He radiates from it a ray of light in the consciousness of a group of His chosen ones, while causing them to be silent about defining it and helpless to transmit it."

MM: *Yet in the enlightened master we can see, know, and feel this silence. Enlightened beings radiate this silence toward us to heal the chaos of our minds and to draw us closer to the state of grace.*

AH: I remember meeting an old woman in Tiruvannamalai, in south India. She had suffered tremendously when young, lost many members of her family in a tragic accident and finally come to a state of suicidal desperation. She went to Ramana Maharshi, who happened to be alone in the small room where he gave darshan, and started to cry, telling him the story of her life. The Maharshi said nothing and went on saying nothing. Slowly the woman stopped crying, stopped talking and just sat with him, gazing into his eyes. She told me that at that moment, light filled the room, and her heart was opened as if by the most delicate spear, running right through the center. This meeting opened in her a bliss she never dreamt could exist, streaming from his compassion. After that, she never talked to the Ramana but stayed by his side for thirty years. Everything she needed, all the food for her soul, had been communicated to her through that silence.

MM: *Language would have blocked that direct transmission of love.*

AH: Words simply don't apply beyond a certain point. Explanations can not heal us. What all of us need is an experience of unconditional and extreme love. Silence is that love. The supreme masters, whatever their teachings, always finally communicate the power of that love directly through silence. Just as in human love, it is not what is said that is sacred, but the wind that passes in looks, touch and solitude that intoxicates.

MM: *The unheard melodies.*

AH: Yes. Thinking of the power of enlightened silence, I come to a story about Milarepa. One day, a robber came to a cave where this thin, crazy-looking man was meditating. The robber stole everything that he possessed, his pot, his bowl, a couple scraps of money that people had left, and slipped away down the mountainside. Suddenly, Milarepa ran after him, naked, holding out the robe he'd been wearing. He didn't *say* anything; he just held out the tattered robe with love burning in his eyes and body. The robber fell at Milarepa's feet and became one of his greatest disciples. The Crucifixion takes place in silence. There are no words in the end; there is only an act.

MM: *No words, only an act, a transfiguring act.*

AH: The holy live in a dimension of total action, one with the sacred power of silence. They are silence acting, silence speaking, silence moving, silence healing.

MM: *The Buddha never defined nirvana. He only gave negative pointers, not this, not that. More than any other mystical technology, it seems to me that Buddhism pays tribute to the dynamic power of emptiness and silence to initiate.*

AH: The Buddha was walking toward the end of his life in an autumn park with his monks. He stooped and picked up a handful of dry leaves and said, "this is what I have said." After a pause, he pointed to the sea of dry leaves stretching as far as anyone could see in all directions, "and that is what I have not said."

The Zen master Bodhidharma was leaving his disciples for the last time. He asked four of them the question, "What is truth?" The first replied that truth is not in the scripture and not in words. Bodhidharma smiled and said to him, "You have my skin." The second replied that truth has to be experienced, it is not a concept. To him, Bodhidharma said, "You have my flesh." The third disciple replied that truth is when you are not, when the ego totally vanishes. Bodhidharma said, "You have my bones." Then he turned and asked the fourth disciple, Huikojo. Huikojo just gazed at him, fell down at his feet and remained silent. Bodhidharma bent down, raised him, hugged him and said, "You have my marrow. I will leave you all I have." To a question about truth, only silence can be the answer.

MM: *There comes a moment in every journey with a master when the master takes away the disciple's words and plunges the disciple into silence. The power of silence slowly breaks all his or her habits of definition, dissolves everything the disciple thinks he or she knows.*

AH: Silence is the real power, the power of the Real. The flowers, trees and mountains grow in silence. The Tao is silent. All things shift and move and die held in the arms of an infinite silence. Through our devotion, masters bestow on us the extraordinary power of the released mind and divinized will, that flowers in the silence of their and our love. This power is what the transformed child of the Divine radiates naturally, as the rose perfumes the air around it, and the grass reflects the sunlight. "*Omnis terra te adorat*"; the whole earth is adoring the Divine in silence.

It is the silence of this adoration that finally stills the mind of Thomas Aquinas. After writing the *Summa Theologiae*, Thomas had a vision at a Mass in Naples. The sky opened, and his mind was flooded with divine light. He gave up work altogether, realizing that everything he said fell absurdly short of the glory he had witnessed.

You can look at this incident two ways: either as God showing the futility of all human works, or as a dazzled silence being the reward for Thomas's life of devotion and learning.

MM: *If only our civilization could grasp that the end of learning is silence.*

AH: Until we do, we will only become more and more chaotic. Let us imagine what a true sacred education might be like. All the different disciplines of the mind in a sacred education would be tuned to and by the silence beyond the mind. Psychology would enable people to enter God's silence. Philosophy would end in the irradiation of the mind by silence. Literature would immerse readers in the meditative silence it emerged from. Mathematics would guide scientists to contemplation of the silence out of which numbers are born. What wonders would astrophysicists discover if their minds were attuned to the silence? An initiation into silence would be at the core of all disciplines, and this would bring us wisdom and peace in all activities, the wisdom and peace of the Mother.

In the silence of the Mother, of the light she is and has brought down, an immense sacred mystery is at work. Her silence is helping to bring in a new world, one which has nothing whatever to do with the noisy definitions that cause aggression, the hierarchies that cause elitism or the religious dogmas that separate. The Mother teaches in silence because she embodies the sacred heart of the universe and the silence of the ground from which all manifestation arises. The Mother teaches in silence because she wants to take us into God directly, beyond mind or concepts, initiate us directly into divine love and divine wisdom. If we allow ourselves to be led by silence from love to love, from vision to vision, the day comes when, as the Dzogchen masters say, through our eyes "the immaculate will look naturally at itself." The child sees and knows the Mother light in the ground of being and merges with it, to reemerge clothed in its radiance and empowered to play seriously in the world to transform it.

Enlightenment is knowing that the Mother is always in the room, and that her tender, enveloping, omnipotent silence is the ground and radiant life-spring of your Self and all things. Realization is knowing that her silent love is directed entirely toward you and toward every being, now and always. What would a love so extreme do but fall silent?

The divine light of the Mother is raining her grace on the world and the Mother is doing everything in her power to open our hearts to this light. This vast silent power of light will, if we let, if we open, transform us and our world.

> *Salutations to Her who keeps all the worlds under her sway*
> *Salutations to Her who grants all our desires*
> *Salutations to Her whose form is existence-knowledge-bliss*
> *Salutations to Her who is not limited by space and time*
> *Salutations to Her who is present in all as the inner controller*
> *Salutations to Her who casts her spell on all.*

—From the Sri Lalita Sahasranama

POSTSCRIPT

by Andrew Harvey

Now the Lord is with them in every alteration, performing an unimaginable work in them hour after hour. If only they knew they would not withdraw from Him even for the moment of a wink. For the Lord does not withdraw from them at any time.

—Al-Hallaj

There is one way and one way only, I believe, that the planet can be saved in time—and that is through a massive worldwide transformation which is simultaneously spiritual and practical, mystical and political. Turning to the light is not, in itself, enough. We have also to act as humble tireless agents of the light, with the light in us, behind us, inspiring and guiding us, to act on all possible spiritual and practical fronts, wisely, calmly and very, very fast.

What is needed is a worldwide, highly organized, spiritual civil disobedience movement. Millions of ordinary people all over the world must take to the streets, if at all possible and as long as possible nonviolently, and simply demand no more destruction of the environment, no more inner and outer pollution, no more mad expenditures on lethal and horrifying weapons. We have had enough. If this worldwide movement of calm inspired protest does not organize itself soon, what can turn the madness of the politicians and corporation leaders around? They are lost in their dream of power, and we must shake them awake.

But for such a movement to arise, there must be millions of people who love the world and are willing to risk everything, their jobs, their reputations, even, in the final analysis, death itself, and spiritual and civic leaders of all kinds willing to tell the world the truth and stake everything on leading the world out of its immense darkness.

There is still just enough time, and with the avatars and masters here and the presence on earth of the light of the Mother, anything is still possible. But very, very soon, time will run out.

If these words mean anything real to you, turn to the light, dedicate yourself to the fight for the future, and start to change everything now. The Divine is waiting to give us all at all times and in all conditions every possible help.

Andrew Harvey was the youngest Fellow ever elected to Oxford University. Born in India in 1952, he was educated in England and graduated from All Souls College in 1971. At age 25, he began his mystical journey: first, meeting with the youthful avatar Mother Meera; later, with Thuksey Rinpoche, whose initiation of the author into Tibetan Buddhism led to Harvey's classic, A *Journey in Ladakh*. The author underwent extraordinary mystical experiences with the Divine Feminine as recorded in *Hidden Journey*. His latest book is A *Way of Passion*, A *Celebration of Rumi*.

Mark Matousek was born in Los Angeles in 1957 and received his M.A. in English from the University of California in 1980. He began his publishing career as Theater Critic for Reuters International, held an editorship at *Newsweek Magazine*, and was Senior Editor at *Interview* for three years under the late artist-publisher Andy Warhol. In 1986, Matousek resigned from *Interview* to accompany Andrew Harvey to Germany, where he met Mother Meera. Back in the U.S., he began a new career as a free-lance journalist, as Contributing Editor first to *Common Boundary* and then to *Details Magazine*. He is currently working on his memoirs to be published in spring, 1996 by G.P. Putnam & Sons.